Speak Out with Marge

…and you'll be gladder that you're alive

Marge Caldwell
with Amelia Bishop

To Pat—
My special love
to you!
Marge

Scripture quotations marked TLB are from *The Living Bible, Paraphrased* (Wheaton: Tyndale House Publishers, 1971) and are used by permission.

Subject Headings: CHRISTIAN LIFE

Printed in the United States of America

Preface

So many times God answers prayer in a more glorious and exciting way than we'd even asked for! So it was with my weekly radio program "Speak Out with Marge," in Houston on Station KXYZ.

I do a lot of speaking for chapels and assemblies on high school and college campuses. Usually I am invited to be interviewed on radio or TV programs when I go. On such an occasion I found myself the guest on a noonday radio show in San Antonio, Texas, for Dorothy Mae Waldron on Christian radio. I was delighted to do it, and as she and I sat outside the control room waiting for our turn to go on, I exclaimed: "Oh, how I'd *love* to do something like this in Houston! Wouldn't it be great to be able to talk about the Lord like this?"

"Have you ever asked the Lord for it?" she asked.

"Oh, no!" I replied. "You see, he's given me so much I haven't the nerve to ask for something else!"

Then she prayed for the program about to begin and thanked the Lord for the program he would give me in his time. I nearly fainted but I recovered to apologize to the Lord for bothering him about this! My faith is tremendous!

I returned home and, in my usual way, prepared to help the Lord answer my prayer! I dressed up and visited all the radio and TV stations, fully expecting someone to be standing on the corner beckoning me to come in and perform. No one did! In fact, no one seemed to know that I was supposed to have a program! So I decided to just let the Lord do it all by himself!

Two years passed, and I completely forgot about it! Then one day I met a young lady who had just joined our church, and we visited about our dreams and goals. I shared with Lyndol my dream for a program, and God used her to open the door to this dream. She was program coordinator for Station KXYZ!

One day the phone rang. The voice on the other end said: "This is KXYZ, and we wanted to know if you would audition for two sixty-second segments for radion, one on poise and one on personality!"

I said I'd try, because I hardly thought I could blow it. I can barely say my name in sixty seconds! I taped the two, and they told me to wait. In a few minutes a man came out and asked me to come in. He was the station program director.

"What would you do if you had a thirty-minute program on our station?" he asked.

"Why, I'd fall down and froth at the mouth," I muttered!

"Mrs. Caldwell, go home and prepare two thirty-minute programs," he said "and one must be an answer to a letter from a high school dropout on drugs and the other an answer to a letter from a woman who feels that all the romance has gone out of her marriage."

I left the room almost speechless and went home and worked on the two programs. I had the eerie feeling you get when you know God is up to something and you're vitally involved! The next day I returned, and they taped the two programs. I waited, and then was ushered in to the general manager's office.

"What are you going to call your program?" he asked.

"I beg your pardon?" I answered.

"We are going to give you a Sunday night program on our station," he answered.

I was actually shaking all over! God *did* do it all by himself! But I was paralyzed with fear as I spoke to him. This was probably going to be the shortest radio program in history, but I had to get something straight! I told him that many times in speaking to school assemblies I would be asked not to mention Jesus' name. I could say God or Lord, but not Jesus. I think Jesus is the cure for all human ills and problems, and I did not think I could talk about him week after week and never mention his Name.

"Are you a Baptist?" he asked.

I meekly answered that I was!

"I'm a Catholic," he laughed, "and I'm tired, too, of not being able to mention Jesus' name. You are free to say anything about him you want to!"

For nearly four years now I have had the beautiful privilege of talking to my radio audience about how Jesus loves them! We call my program "Speak Out with Marge."

One day someone said: "Marge, why don't you write a book and make it a collection of your radio programs?"

So the idea was born, and here it is! If God can use anything in this book to help anyone, I will be eternally grateful! I'm so excited when I think of what he can do if we will just be available, and believe.

My deepest appreciation to Amelia Bishop (Mrs. Ivaloy Bishop) whom God used over and over in the preparation of this book in editing and working tirelessly! She was a beautiful answer to prayer too!

And, of course, I want to thank our daughter, Gay, for her tireless task of typing! It was a labor of love and I am really grateful!

To Gay and Chuck, Jr., our wonderful
son and daughter

God gives us many gifts in a lifetime that bless us . . . but the
most wonderful gift that he has given us is the gift of our children! They have brought us love, laughter, excitement, and yes,
a few tears . . . but their beautiful lives have given us "a little
touch of heaven on earth!" Chuck and I are proud to have been
their parents!

Contents

1
You—A Fascinating Woman/ A Charming Man

Let's talk about a fascinating woman and a charming man. To lead us into the area, let me hold forth on one of my favorite subjects—a man named Chuck. I like him. He's my husband.

Now, Chuck and I met each other at Rice University—oh, my soul—at least a hundred years ago. We fell madly, excitingly in love, and at that time, things were a little different. For Chuck, I mean. He had a whole lot of hair and no stomach. Now everything has been rearranged, so to speak. But I really do like that old boy!

And speaking of hair, I came in one day, really complaining. It was pouring down rain, and I didn't know what to do with my hair. I was having a fit, a living fit. "Oh, Chuck," I moaned. "Look at my hair! It's just hanging there!"

"Now, honey, don't knock it," he replied. "At least it's hanging on!"

Chuck has just a little bit of hair around the edges of his head. He has put on maybe a few pounds since we fell in love (and I have too) but I want to tell you we've been married—happily married— for thirty-seven wonderful years.

Sometimes when I tell young people we've been married this long and we are still in love, they look at me like "My soul! She's old enough to die!" But we really have had a great married life, and for that we're grateful to God and thrilled to have been able to spend so much time together.

Now I'm going to let Chuck talk to you. I want you to know a man's thoughts on a fascinating woman. You say this is not you?

Well, it could be. Stay with me.

My husband is a successful executive in the oil business. He's thrown with all kinds of people during the day and in the evenings as well. He has to be a gracious employer, a thoughtful host. He is a kind person—an observant person—and I thought he would be someone who could tell us from the masculine viewpoint about a fascinating woman. When he gets through, I want to talk with you about what a truly charming man would be like. I want to share with you some of the viewpoints (not all my own thinking, but the viewpoints of women and girls whom I have interviewed over a period of years) about the charming man. What do we women really want in our men? But let's start with Chuck—and his views of women.

"Chuck, I just feel so good looking at you and seeing those blue eyes!" Girls, I wish you could see him. . . . he makes me melt and run down in my shoes!

"Marge, thank you! I *do* like the things you've said about me—most of them. It's true I do have a little less hair, and a little more waistline, but I'm still not the one in the family who gets mistaken for Phyllis Diller! And now to my subject: the fascinating woman ."

I asked him my first question, "Chuck, in speaking of a woman who is truly fascinating, is it necessary that she be a raving beauty?"

"It isn't necessary . . . but on the other hand, it wouldn't hurt anything."

I thought a moment. "You mean some of us get born beautiful, and the rest of us just get born? Is that what you mean?"

He smiled. "That's what I mean. It isn't truly necessary that she be beautiful. Actually, the term 'fascinating' may be misleading. Fascination has always lent a little bit of mystery, and I think this actually isn't necessary. The fascinating woman is really a friendly person. She's a combination of graciousness and charm. ·And graciousness you acquire when you practice kindness, cheerfulness, and good manners. Charm comes from an interest in and a love for other people.

"When I think of the fascinating women I have known," Chuck

went on, "they were lovely people. But it wasn't because of their looks; it was because of their manners, their dispositions. It was their personality—their interest in other people. You felt it was a pleasure to be around them, a pleasure to know them. You always felt better after visiting with them."

I mulled over what he was saying. (After all, he could be trying to tell me something!) "Then what you are expressing, Chuck, is the idea that their physical beauty is not the most important thing. But how about neatness and good grooming? Where does that enter in?"

His reply was direct. "Many women who are not actually attractive make themselves appear so by working at the job. They are careful in their clothes and their makeup, and they are neat. One of the things that will turn a man off the quickest is noticing that a person is untidy or has the appearance of being unclean. This may be the first prerequisite: To be neat, to be tidy in dress, makeup, and similar things. And there's something too about smell—a woman ought to smell good!"

I made a mental note to buy some more perfume! "What about the mental aspect of fascinating?" I asked. "You hear so much about women's lib . . . I tell you, I don't want to be liberated from anything. I'm having too much fun just being a woman. But there are those who do not go along with that idea. How do men really feel about intelligent women—highly educated women?"

He hesitated a moment. "I think I'd say it depends on how she uses her intelligence and her education. Here, a woman is no different from a man. We see so many people who have all the education in the world, and they like for you to know it. They enjoy making themselves appear more intelligent than anyone. I think it's wonderful to see a woman who is intelligent, well-read, and well-educated. She can be interesting in her conversation, and yet she does not give the impression of looking down on anyone or of being smarter than anyone. So, education is a wonderful thing, but it can also be a dangerous thing."

In the back of my mind ran something about a little knowledge being a dangerous thing.

Chuck continued, "It can be dangerous because a person—man or woman—can be an educational snob."

He paused, and I said what I was thinking. (Speaking of danger—it's really dangerous for him to pause when we're talking together.) "I get the impression that the more you really know, the more humble you become—because you realize how much you don't know! It's that way about the Bible. Once you realize how little you know, you start reading, and the more you know, the more you realize how much you don't know—if you know what I mean!"

Chuck sighed, "I'm trying, Marge—I'm trying."

I slowed down so as not to sound like a 33 rpm recording on a 45 sound track. "Let's go on to the emotional side of life. You know—that's where a woman lives. You men are so factual. You add two and two, and you get four every time. Women add two and two, and get five one day and three the next—depending on how we feel about it." "I know I'm emotional . . ." (Chuck opened his mouth but I kept right on talking anyway). "Maybe that's one of the things that makes us interesting to you men. You don't understand us, but you love us anyway."

Chuck added another thought. "Women are that way, but also there are some men who add two and two and get four, then don't want to face it, to act upon it. So we're also a little bit odd in some of these things. But back to the emotional side of a woman. I think herein actually lies the charm and the depth of many women. You love a person who is unselfish. You love a person who is kind and cheerful, who is smiling, enthusiastic, and optimistic. You love someone who is genuinely interested in other people. All of these are emotional aspects—you show how you feel! When you see a combination of intelligence and kindness and interest, then you have a very interesting and a fascinating person. If you have someone who is widely traveled and widely read and can talk well on many subjects and yet they take time to find out about you and to discuss your interests and make you feel like you also are well acquainted on a lot of things—this is genuine interest and kindness. This is true fascination."

I followed along with him. "It is coming through to me that what we call 'fascination' is really in large measure actually 'unselfishness.' It's to be interested in other people. Everything you have said points to the fact that a fascinating woman has to be someone interested in other people. This is unselfishness. Well, we've talked about a lot of things. Do you think a fascinating woman needs a sense of humor?"

Chuck chuc . . . (I almost said "Chuck chuckled," but that would be too much strain on anyone's sense of humor.) Let's just say he laughed softly. "Very definitely," he answered. "One of the most important things a person should have is a sense of humor."

"Define it."

"Well, it's not so much getting tickled at other people. It's to be able to see the humor in situations whether it's someone else or you involved. When you can laugh at yourself, it means you can step out of yourself and see the situation—your mind isn't just focused on you. That ties in again with unselfishness."

I followed him. (And this is not always easy for me.) "Well, before we tie it all together, let's touch on one other area. Does it matter if a woman has any spiritual depth or not?"

"Very definitely," he answered quickly. "I do not feel that a person—man or woman—can be an entire person, a charming person, a fascinating personality with depth without a spiritual depth—a basic belief in Jesus Christ as Savior. No matter how widely traveled they are, or how widely read, or how well-educated . . . no matter how many possessions they have, or how successful they might be, if they do not have Christ as a basis of their life, I don't feel they can be a genuinely charming and fascinating person."

I had a thought I wanted to share: "You know, Chuck, Jesus was the author of charm, beauty, and inward radiance. Often in my charm classes I meet girls and women who have all of the physical attributes in the world that a person could want, all the mental capabilities, emotional balance, and yet they will be absolutely blank where the most important area of their life is."

There flashed through my mind a bittersweet truth. Girls can be taught to model, they can be taught to be charming—mechanically. But a walking doll may not be a living doll. If the beauty and radiance are not there within, there is an emptiness about the face. Often I've thought, If Christ were added to this, wouldn't it be the most wonderful thing that ever was? For with him, come beauty and radiance—and they shine through.

Chuck read my mind, as usual. (Assuming, of course, there is something to read.) "Let's cap the conversation by saying this: If a fascinating woman has Christ, she is even more fascinating." He paused. "But enough from me. Let's turn this thing around and talk about men. Charming men. I want to hear what you have to say."

To talk never has been hard for me. "Well, to begin with (though I seldom start at the beginning) the thing that I think should be most dominant in the life of a charming man is something we have already touched on—a concern for other people. Sometimes it's called an 'outgoing personality' but I don't know that I like that because most of us are too outgoing anyway, in our day and age."

Chuck's silence made me go on hastily: "Seriously, the charming man has a love and concern for others, and it runs deep. He is concerned about every area of their lives, not just the point at which his life touches theirs. He makes them feel like he is interested in them as individual persons. And by doing this, he puts them at ease. Let me give you an example:

"Long ago I was at a dinner meeting where Dr. William Hendricks of Fort Worth was in attendance. Dr. Hendricks has four degrees that I know of; he speaks several languages; he has the most beautiful command of the English language I've ever heard; and his vocabulary is absolutely stupendous! As I heard him speaking before the meal, I thought, Oh, my soul, if I sit by him at dinner, I'll die. I won't be able to say one word to that man who is so intelligent, and so beautifully educated. I really worried about it.

"Of course it happened. Our fears have a way of catching us. I was his dinner partner for that evening. Dr. Hendricks was without a doubt one of the most charming people I have ever met. I was prepared to be ill at ease as I sat down there. I thought, I wonder what I can talk intelligently to him about? I certainly wasn't about to bring up the weather as most people do when they don't know what else to talk about.

"Before I could do a thing, or say a thing, he turned around and said, 'Mrs. Caldwell, tell me about you.'

"Well, that put me at my ease. At least I did know about me. I didn't know about him, but I knew about me. We began to talk, and I believe that was one of the most rewarding and stimulating hour and a half conversations I have ever had. He shared because he was interested. He didn't talk down to me, in spite of his education and his intelligence level. He talked *to* me, and it was so interesting. He was so stimulating, and he had been so many places. I enjoyed talking to him so much. When I left, I reflected on what a charming man he was. He cared about his dinner partner, he cared to the extent that he was trying to talk with me and to share with me. I learned much from him, and yet, when we left, he said, 'Thank you for sharing some of your life and your mind with me.' I thought, If only you knew how afraid I was when I sat down here! But I had been so stimulated by his conversation that all fear left me."

Chuck summed up my ramblings for me: "You've covered some aspects of the charming man: how he puts others at ease; how he makes others feel important; how he converses easily, but keeps himself in the background. But let's bring the subject in the front door, so to speak. Let's talk about the man of the house who wants to be charming but also wants to be a man. Isn't there a time when you women want this also? Does a man lose his charm if he asserts himself?"

I had no trouble with that one. "Not at all! I think God intended for the man to be the head of the house. I've often said to many young people that a woman who will nag her husband, or not let him be the head of the house, will never have a truly happy home. God intended for the man to be the head of the house. He told the woman to love and honor her husband. He told the man to love his wife like Christ loved the church and gave his life for it. I really think a man needs to be the head of the house. Now, I don't mean the type of person who would stomp in and demand 'Where is my dinner? Is my dinner ready?' A man must earn the love and respect of his wife and the children in the home. He has every right to expect a wife to put him first. And I have a sort of 'thing' about this. I think a man and a woman should put each other first in the family relationship. The children grow up and leave, and there the two of you are! Chuck may have forgotten this, but I haven't. We were driving back to Midland after putting our youngest in the University of Texas, and he looked at me and said: 'Marge, I hope we still like each other, don't you?' We were starting back home again, starting a brand-new life in one sense of the word—just the two of us again starting back where we started years ago."

Another angle on the home front is this: It is important that the children see Dad lead out in their prayer life. A wife must let her husband—or urge him to, if need be—lead out in spiritual areas. A charming man, like a fascinating woman, must not only have a spiritual side to life—he must also let it be seen.

Chuck interrupted my mental monologue. "You believe the charming man has spirit, don't you? In an effort to get along, surely he doesn't play Mr. Milk-toast."

"Not at all. But when the charming man and his wife disagree or when he disagrees with anyone—and he has to or he would be a jellyfish—he talks it over with them personally. At home, he would disagree with his wife, but not in front of the children. That's called consideration, and it's also called security—the little children with the big eyes aren't all shook up because Mom and Dad are going at it!"

That's about it. You do these things—or don't do them—in order to be charming, to be fascinating. That's a by-product, like happiness. You try giving yourself away, and suddenly you find that you are happy. And, incidentally, in the process, you have become a fascinating woman, or a charming man.

It's nothing new. It had its basis in a Man who walked the Galilean hills some two thousand years ago. He talked about "losing your life to find it." The person who loses himself in others finds that life is fascinating (and she is fascinating) or that life has a wonderfully deep charm (and he has that charm).

Why not start now. Look at that man you married. ("My soul! Is he the one?" Yes, he is.) Or look at that wife of yours—maybe her hair is up in curlers, she has on no makeup, and looks like she just got up from yellow jaundice. ("Did I marry her?") Yes, you did.

Put your arms around each other, and be thankful for the Christian home you have.

This is where it all begins.

2
A Sense of Humor—
Get Out of Yourself

Hello out there. Did you run across anything exciting today . . . like some magic keys maybe?

No—I'm not kidding—I'm serious! At any rate, what I have to say is exciting because it works like magic. And it's a key because it opens doors you never thought you'd be able to crack. What am I talking about? A sense of humor. It works for you and for those around you. It's excellent therapy. It makes the happy days seem happier; it broadens the silver lining around the edge of any dark cloud.

All my life I've heard, "You must have a great sense of humor," and I sort of took it as a matter of course. I noticed that I could stand on a street corner, and if someone fell down I might have an almost uncontrollable desire to start laughing. In fact, a few times I have, and it did not add a great deal to my popularity. I noticed that I was seeing the humor in lots of incidents, but not particularly in my own life. If it happened to Marge Caldwell, that was something else again.

Let me share three happenings with you and show you what I mean. From these three I learned some very important lessons about this almost undefinable something we call a "sense of humor."

The first came about when I was asked to speak before a civic club in Houston. When the program chairman called me, he indicated that the club was having a banquet to honor their wives. He told me something about what they had in mind and arranged for the date, time, and place. Then he concluded by saying, "Now,

Mrs. Caldwell, be funny!" He made matters worse by saying, "And by the way, this crowd doesn't laugh very easily, but I know you can handle it." Now that'll do something for you! Be funny—but they don't laugh easily!

Well, you don't just press a button and everyone laughs. So I was a little nervous about this whole affair to begin with. And Chuck didn't help much. When I told him my concern, he just shrugged his shoulders and said: "No problem, Honey. I've heard all your stuff so many times I know ahead of time where the laugh lines are. I'll start them off by laughing in the right places."

The night of the banquet came, as those things have a way of doing. Chuck and I were getting dressed, and I was very, very quiet. That means one of two things—either I'm sick or I'm nervous. Chuck kept saying: "Now, Marge, don't be nervous—you'll do all right. Just don't be nervous."

You know how it is when your husband hits a nerve. "I am NOT nervous," I screeched. "I am perfectly calm!"

"Then why don't your shoes match?"

I glared at him and went to change one of them.

The trip to the hotel was a very quiet one. Just before we got out of the car, the incident at home forgotten, Chuck said: "Just relax, Honey, and you'll do fine." "I am NOT nervous," I repeated and got out of the car like the Queen of Sheba.

As we were walking down a corridor looking for the banquet room, someone stopped me to say something, and Chuck walked on ahead. When I finished talking, I hurried to catch up with him, and he turned a corner and went through a door. I went in right behind him. He wheeled abruptly to face me, and said, eyeball to eyeball, "Honey, you ARE nervous!"

"I am not," I flipped back, just like a broken record.

He began to laugh, leaned against the wall, and between his ho-ho's sputtered, "If you're not nervous, then what are you doing in the men's room?"

I nearly came unglued. I was in the middle of the men's rest room. I have never been so upset in my whole life. And I want to tell you something else—it's a lot easier to get in a men's rest room than it is to get out. Chuck wasn't helping any, either. This husband who had promised to "love, honor, and cherish" me just stood there, leaning up against the wall, weak from laughter.

But just standing there helped not at all. So I remembered what I always told my girls in charm school: "When you're in a bind, just hold your head high and walk out." That's exactly what I did, or tried to do. In the process, two men were coming in and almost knocked me down. I looked them straight in the eye and said, "Hello . . . pardon me, please," and swept out the door.

They went on in. Chuck told me later they all laughed together, and then one said, "They're taking over our rest rooms now." The other commented: "Did you see her acting like Madame Queen and saying 'Hello?' Man, I can't stand that! What a repulsive cat!" They said a little more, and one asked Chuck, "Did you see her?"

"Yeah, I saw her," Chuck replied. "Man, wasn't she something?" Still laughing, he walked on out the door and met me on the outside. "Those two guys really worked you over, Marge."

Well, we found our banquet hall and went on up to the head table which was elevated by a platform from the rest of the guests. The crowd began to drift in to be seated. I began looking around and nearly died. At the table closest to us were those same two men with their wives. They hadn't seen me and didn't know I was with Chuck; they were just sitting there talking. After the meal, they began to gaze about, and one of them looked in my direction. He did a double take, gasped, and then wheeled to whisper something to his friend. They both looked. I just waved real big, and said, "Hi, there!" They kind of halfway waved back with sick grins on their faces, looking from me to Chuck, and from Chuck to me.

I had fun that night, and I didn't have to worry about making anyone laugh. These two men turned out to be the real nuts in the crowd and excellent sports, also. I began by relating the rest room incident and all the things they had said to my husband. Although their faces were red, they laughed louder than anyone. Everyone had a good time. They knew how to laugh at themselves, and thus, turn an embarrassing situation into a humorous one. They were a good example for me—and I needed it later.

The second incident could have been life's most embarrassing moment. We had not been in Houston too long, and my husband had changed companies. We did not know many of his new employees—husbands and wives—so we thought a company dinner would be a nice gesture at this point. Also, his secretary would be leaving the company in a few weeks and we thought that a going-away present would add a festive note to the occasion. It was fun planning it all—the date, time, menu, gift—the whole bit.

Suddenly the day was upon us.

Now I really have to work to prepare a dinner for ten. For some kinds of people, preparation is a complete joy. But I must confess that for me it is just horrible. Nothing ever seems to come out right. The house must be clean, and when I work at that, I wear the most comfortable attire I can imagine. This particular day it consisted of a pair of hot-pants (the same thing that young people today call "hot pants"), some slides, a battered old T-shirt, no makeup, and my hair rolled up in bobby pins. I looked something like an old Mexican gourd with a chicken wire helmet. Mother had loaned me her maid, Tillie, who could absolutely work miracles out of mistakes. She was the one who was going to perform a miracle for me today by her cooking. It was nearly five o'clock and dinner was well underway. The house was spotless (at least where you could see), and Chuck was going to bring Jerry's gift with him. I sat down to wipe a little dust from the bottom of the chair. Whoops! I felt something give and began to inspect. My shorts were not new, and the extra strain was just a little much. But why worry, I thought, the back seam just gave a little, and besides it was almost time to get dressed.

At that moment Chuck came bounding into the house, running over with energy and good humor. He never walks anywhere like an average person. He just sort of bounds into a room.

He was all smiles and good cheer, but I didn't see the package. "Where's Jerry's gift?" I asked.

"Oh, Marge, I forgot it," was all he could say as he turned the color of an old ripe banana. And do you know what he said next? Can you guess?

"Now look Marge—we only have thirty minutes to get back downtown and pick it up before the store closes. You'll have to circle the block, and I'll run in and get it."

"Circle the block? Like this? Not on your life," I squealed. "Chuck, I wouldn't be caught dead like this. And besides that I've torn my . . ." Before I could finish he broke in. "Oh never mind! Who'll see you? Come on!" Since that was my master's voice, the next thing I knew we were on our way to town.

We did make it in all that traffic by 5:25 P.M. That was a miracle, too, except that everyone else was going home. I was to let him out at the store, go down on Main Street to Texas, turn right (one-way streets do complicate matters), and pick him up behind the jewelers.

Well, everything went according to schedule. At first, that is. He got out, I drove one block and stopped for a red light. Just then an excruciating thought crossed my mind, What if the motor would stop . . . I would just die looking like this. The traffic was electric. Everyone was hurrying, cars and busses alike, bumper to bumper. Crowds were everywhere, whistles blowing, brakes screeching.

I sat there waiting for the light to turn green. Then it happened. You won't believe this, but my motor actually did die. For a minute I thought I would too, and then the next moment, I wished I had. Horns honked, people screamed, whistles blew, and there I sat. And sat. The starter wouldn't even turn over, but my stomach certainly did. Finally after several changes in the light, the man behind me screamed, "When the light changes, I'll push you to get you started."

Now, I'm not much of a driver—I never have been—so you should have seen me. Our car really had to be pushed to start. Well, he pushed, I jerked, but nothing happened. By that time we were in the middle of the next block. Before I knew what had actually happened, that man drove up beside me and screamed, "Lady, you're on your own. Good luck!" He had this big grin on his face, and then he was gone.

Now the traffic really began to jell. You couldn't move a car for two blocks in any direction. People who were standing on the curb waiting for the bus about a block behind me did one of two things: they either leered at me and muttered to their friends or laughed and pointed at me. At this moment I was absolutely stunned. All of a sudden I thought of Chuck. I think I came very close to hating him for a moment. If I could have just gotten my hands on him!

People are wonderful, and I usually love them. But when you're in that kind of a jam, you see a completely new side of human nature. Car problems do terrible things to even rational human beings. I couldn't think of a thing to do in that indescribable situation. There was nothing to do, I decided. I might as well use the time to improve myself. I guess I could take the bobby pins out of my hair. Now don't ask me why I thought of my hair—I just wasn't thinking at all. I started jerking pins out right and left, throwing them out the window, in the front seat, out the window, in the back seat, on the floor—in general, just straight up. Then I began running my fingers through my hair which made me look very much like a porcupine. At this point, I looked in the mirror, and you-know-who was coming. The policeman, of course. He edged his way over to me and my car (and that took some edging), his eyes flashing, his mouth in a cold, thin line. "Lady," he clipped out, "did you come downtown at 5:30 in the afternoon, tie up traffic in every direction, just to take your hair down?"

I gulped and swallowed and tried to cover my lap with my hands and sputtered and finally managed to say, "Well, you see, sir, my car won't start." Now wasn't that a pearl of wisdom?

He glared and screeched over the honking autos, "Go in there and call somebody!" And he pointed to a shoe store that was right there in front of me.

I tried to explain that I wasn't dressed properly . . . that I had a slight tear in the back of my shorts, and that I didn't have any

makeup on, but I don't think I told him a thing. Any moron could
know by looking at me that I surely wasn't prepared. Looking back,
I believe I detected a twinkle in his eye, but the only thing I saw at
that time was the glare. What in the world could I do? I didn't
want to go in the store past those staring, laughing people and use
the telephone, but I had to. In desperation, I turned and said to him,
"I don't have any money." And he actually got his hand down in
his pocket and threw a dime in my hand and said: "Now then! Go
in there!"

With one hand holding the torn seam in my shorts and the other
hand with the dime in it, I started through that crowd. You should
have seen them—you would think they had never seen a woman
dressed like this in such a predicament. Well, I wedged my way
through the door of the shoe store and I passed one of the employees who had come out to the scene of the crime. I thought to
myself, He must have had a hair-brained wife at home and has a com-
passionate heart, because he looked at me with real pity in his eyes.
"Lady, would you like to use the telephone?"

"Yes, sir," I whispered, thinking I was going to make things
worse by crying. But somehow I got by without tears and went
to the telephone, dialed my father's office, and waited. Now
Mother and Daddy had an office two blocks away, and I hoped I
could reach them before they left for home. Man, I hoped Mother
would answer. She's faster in emergencies. Dad always has to have
all the details before he can make any kind of a decision, and I just
wasn't in the mood. But Daddy answered.

"Hello," he said in a booming voice. I just asked in a crisp voice
to put Mother on the phone, please. And for once he did just that.
Now my mother was very much a lady—every inch of her—right
down to her white gloves and hat. I have always been the bane of
her existence. I either had on one glove, or my hose didn't match,
or my makeup wasn't on right, or something. She warned me by
saying, "Marge, someday you're going to be caught like that, and
you'll be so embarrassed." Of course, I thought to myself, It won't
happen to me!

Mother's sweet voice came over the phone. "Hello, dear. How are you?"

I said in a calm voice: "Now Mother, listen carefully. My car is stalled in front of a shoe store" . . . and I told her where. "Chuck is waiting for me to pick him up," and I described where he was. "Get in your car, pick him up, and get over here to push my car."

She exclaimed, "What a shame, Honey. What do you have on?"

Close to tears, I just screamed, "Nothing, Mother."

There was a long, loud silence. You see, Mother never knows exactly what I might do, and I think she was really frightened. "I'll be right there, Honey," she answered with real panic in her voice.

Meanwhile, out in the street, my friend the policeman had directed traffic so that he cleared a space of about three car lengths in front of my car. I crept out, ran through people who still laughed and stared, and crawled into my car.

"Did you get somebody?" he demanded.

"Yes, I did," I whispered, and thoughts began to pour into my mind: I'm going to cry. No, I think I'll just scratch Chuck's eyes out with my bare hands when he gets here. I could just see the headlines in the paper the next day: "Woman jerks husband's head off before gaping throng."

Finally, in the rearview mirror, I saw Dad's car. Chuck was driving. He pulled up slowly and stopped. Oh no—he was going to let Mother push us. He crawled in our car, took the wheel without saying a word, and I thought, If he laughs, I'll scream at the top of my voice.

Mother began to push us. And you know—she's worse than I am. The car jumped and jerked and sputtered, and then miracle of all miracles—it finally started. We finally got out of that traffic and found ourselves on the way home.

Chuck looked at me as I cried quietly. I had to cry. He just didn't understand. Finally he said: "Honey, I'm sorry. But don't cry. You know what it does to you, and I want you to look your best tonight."

Other people can cry, and their eyes just glisten and they look so dewey-eyed. But when I cry I look like someone who had just gotten over yellow jaundice. So I decided to quit that silly stuff. All of a sudden I thought of the dinner and got sick all over again. It was now 6:30 and they were coming at 7:30. I prayed that Tillie would hold the fort down and take things in hand. I made Chuck promise that he would never mention this episode to a soul, and he vowed that there wasn't one soul who could drag it out of him.

Now if you have ever had a dinner where the employees and their wives do not know each other, you'll understand what I'm going to tell you. Chuck and I had rather die than have a dull party. We'd just do anything to break the ice to make it informal and fun.

Well, the party couldn't seem to get off the ground. The guests had just exhausted the topics of the weather, the news, the sports. What a dull deal. I was desperately trying to think of some hilarious anecdote when suddenly I caught Chuck's eye across the room. His eyes are blue, and they literally dance when he is thinking of something pretty onery to do. "Man—you wouldn't dare!" I muttered to myself.

As his eyes met mine, I detected a look of, "Forgive me, honey, but it's for the good of the cause." And then he began, "Let me tell you something on ole Marge! You should have seen her about 5:30 this afternoon in the middle of town. Our car stopped and it wouldn't start. She was dressed in . . ." and on and on and on he went.

They laughed, they howled. Chuck is a good storyteller, even though sometimes you might not recognize the story. By the time he was through, everyone's jawbone had thawed out. In fact, they all had something they wanted to add to it about their most embarrassing moment. And we laughed until we were almost sick.

Needless to say, it saved the day for our party.

And I might add by way of a postscript—I practically put on my gloves now just to go across the street!

The third incident was also one that was totally unexpected. It happened before we moved from Midland to Houston. Chuck and I had invited an elderly couple (about five years older than we) to come and see the plant where Chuck worked. So we flew down to Houston to pick them up, arriving at the old Houston airport where you had to walk down steps to get your luggage. We were with our friends, the Markhams, waiting for the luggage to be brought from the plane. Mrs. Markham and I were chatting. Now keep in mind I was standing there minding my own business (an interesting reversal of behavior) with a perfectly straight face, talking quietly (so to speak). I hadn't even laughed out loud since we got there. And my hair—well, I had done the best I could. Some of us get born beautiful, and the rest of us just get here. But I had done the best I could with what I had to work with and was just standing there visiting, when a young man walked right up to me, shoved a pencil and piece of paper in my hand, and asked, "May I have your autograph?"

I was shocked out of my mind. "I'm sorry," I said hastily, "you must have made a mistake. I don't believe you want *my* autograph." And I wondered who he thought I was.

"Yes I do," he insisted. "I want to give it to my children."

"Well, I'll be glad to," I said, beginning to feel frustrated. "But my autograph doesn't mean anything. You don't know who I am because I'm not anyone important."

"Now don't try to kid me, lady," he countered. "If you'll give me your autograph, I promise I won't even tell anyone you're here!" He pushed the pencil and paper at me again.

"But I don't care who knows I'm here," I countered. I knew I had called my mother, and she had called my friends. I didn't care who knew. But this didn't impress him! Meanwhile my elderly friend started punching me in the ribs saying, "Go ahead, give it to him!"

"I would," I answered. "But I don't know who he thinks I am."

"Oh don't be coy with me" he finally said in exasperation. "I'd know you anywhere. You're Phyllis Diller!"

I rared back in openmouth amazement. "Phyllis Diller!"

"Of course you are," he grinned at me and winked slyly. "Come on now—just write your name for me."

I turned to go, and he took me by the arm. At that moment Chuck walked up. "What does that man want?"

"Honey," I replied, almost beside myself, "He thinks I'm Phyllis Diller, and he wants my autograph."

Chuck bared his teeth. "She *is* Phyllis Diller," he said, "and I'm Fang!"

"I knew it, I knew it!" The man nearly came unglued. "I knew you were Phyllis Diller!"

And so I couldn't do a thing but write "Phyllis Diller" on that sheet of paper, but underneath it I also wrote "By Marge Caldwell."

Well, we got in the cab, and I was muttering, "Can you imagine that man thinking he had found Phyllis Diller down by the luggage!"

The cab driver only heard the words "Phyllis Diller" and he slammed on his brakes. "I knew it!" he exclaimed. "I knew I'd get her. I knew it!"

And so it went.

Well, to make a short story long, I've never lived that one down.

These are three incidents that have taught me some valuable lessons about this thing we call a sense of humor. Perhaps the first thing we can say is that if you can learn to laugh at yourself—to see yourself as others see you in a humorous situation, it helps you to put things in the right perspective. You have to get outside yourself to do it—to see how it really looks. That's good for all of us.

I think we would also say that when you learn to do this—to laugh at a situation—it lightens your spirit and the spirit of those around you. It's contagious, in a good sort of way.

I guess the third thing you'd say is that it makes the ground level— you're all in it together. And the result of all this? It makes you a more joyous Christian.

Notice how many times the word *joy* appears in the New Testament. We are to be "joyous Christians." This is one way to do it.

3
Can God Really Change a Man?

I want to introduce you to my dear, dear friend, George Wetherell. George and Madelyn (who are to be married soon) are like mine and Chuck's children. We love them just that much! George Wetherell has had a phenomenal, miraculous thing happen to him, and I wanted him to share it with you.

"George, I want you to share with us a little of your life. I think it would be helpful and interesting."

"Well, Marge, I was reared in the little town of Dothan, Alabama, which is about twenty miles from Georgia and twenty miles from Florida. It had about forty thousand people in it and was the type of town that was down really in the "heart of Dixie." My father was a pilot on an army base there. I went to school in Dothan from the first grade on up. It was a continual struggle, I felt, to be accepted there. As few people realize, most of the people on an army base are scattered out over a wide area. There weren't many people around that I could really draw close to. I was trying continually to have friends and be accepted in this little town. I played football, was on the boxing team, and was involved in all sports. I played football all the way through three years of high school. But, it seemed like the more and the harder I tried, the less I succeeded. During football season I had more friends than I could count. At the end of football season, though, all my friends seemed to disappear! I really felt alone. I felt like I just wasn't accepted. My girl friend was a cheerleader, and she was my girl friend during football season. But at the end of the season, she was . . . ."

"She found a basketball player, right?"

"Yes!"

"George, wouldn't you say that this feeling of not quite being accepted is a traumatic experience with young people in their home, or school, or wherever they are?"

"Yes, I'd certainly say that! Because I didn't feel accepted, I strove with all my heart to find peer approval. If I couldn't get it in one place   . ."

'You were going to try someplace else!"

"Right! I was going to be accepted one way or another!"

"That's right. Then you moved to Houston, didn't you? In the meantime, you were in the service before that move, right?"

"Well, my parents had moved to Houston so when I got out of the Navy, I came here. I had been discharged from the Navy, and I felt like I didn't have any place in society. That's a lonely feeling. I'd been 'Red, White and Blue . . . and Mom's Apple Pie' for the United States, but I came back and it was different. I *really* felt alone then. Somehow I began to feel like an outcast. The service was the only place I ever felt that I really belonged. I was really desperate for a belonging feeling. So I joined a motorcycle gang!"

"Here in Houston, George?"

"Yes, here in Houston. This motorcycle gang is stretched all over this nation now. I got into the motorcycle gang, and to achieve approval, I tried to appear tough! I never was really tough or anything like that. I never wanted to be. But I got into the gang, and when I got into one fight, everybody talked it up. Soon somebody picked a fight with me, and I had to back it up! My reputation, a reputation which was 90 percent fictitious, seemed to push me on. Finally, the fiction became less and less, and fact became more and more."

"How tall are you, George?"

"I'm six feet three, and weigh 220 pounds! But let me continue! This type of existence continued for two and a half years. I rode and partied and really tried to achieve acceptance through drink, drugs, and sex. Everything lost its appeal after a while, however. It seemed like the more I drank and was involved in these different things, the more alone I felt. Hate was deep inside of me, and down inside of my chest there was a vacuum that just couldn't be filled."

"George, this is a good place to say that in the chest, in the heart of everyone, there is a God-shaped void, and no one can find happiness until they fill it with him. Don't you agree?"

"It's like trying to put a triangle in a round hole."

"It just won't work, will it? Well, go ahead, George."

"All this continued, and one night I found myself in the middle of a giant gang party. Everyone was drinking and eating barbeque, and I was sitting at a table with a big, juicy piece of barbeque in one hand and a beer in the other. Through the door walked a young man who was clean-cut and well-mannered. With this motorcycle gang, you just didn't walk in clean-cut and well-mannered! He walked over and started handing out what they call 'The Four Spiritual Laws.' This tract shows about the love of God. Well, this young man came in and was handing these out, and everybody was ridiculing him and putting him down. When he got to me, I was going to really put it on him, because I saw him as one of those 'do-good Christians' who's come down here to save us all! When I looked in that man's face, I saw pure love there! He handed me that tract, and when everyone was ready to leap on him, I said, 'Let him go!' This man could have left immediately but he didn't. He looked at all of us, and with big tears rolling down his face, he said, 'You people are riding with the devil. You don't know where you're going, and you don't know where you've been!'

"With that, he just turned and walked out quietly. He never insulted anybody or put anybody down. In pure love he came there."

"That was a dangerous thing to do, wasn't it, George?"

"Yes, particularly with our type of people who are dissatisfied with the world and are looking for things to hate. You see, hate grew in our hearts til' finally we *really* hated people, especially outsiders. Here was an outsider! So it was dangerous!"

"Do you know who he is?"

"I've never found him."

"Wouldn't you like to talk with him someday?"

"I really would!"

"Would you know him if you ever saw him?"

"Yes, I think so."

"How I hope your paths cross someday, and you can tell him
how God used him."

"Well, Marge, when he gave me this tract and left, I sat down in
a corner and opened it up. On the first page it said, 'God loves you.'
Remember, I didn't have any love in my life at that time. On the
last page (you know how you look at the first page and the last
page), it showed two circles. In one circle, it showed a picture
of a chair. It said 'this is your life' and it showed a cross, represent-
ing Christ, on this chair. Everything was order inside this circle of
this person's life. In the other circle, it said 'self' on the top of the
chair, and everything was chaos. I looked at that tract, and then I
looked around me! I saw people leaping on top of tables, fights
going on, drinking, pieces of greasy barbeque being thrown from
one side of the room to the other and I said, *'This* is chaos!' "

"That was a picture of you, wasn't it?"

"That was the way my life felt—chaotic! I didn't know what to
do. Right after that I climbed on a motorcycle and went to look
for this young man. I never found him. For six months I tried
to find him. I went to different churches, and all kinds of different
places. All this time I was judging Christ by Christians who were
staring at me and avoiding me."

"Can't do that, can you, George?"

"You really can't!"

"Well, George, that brings you up to date, about six months later,
when you met two girls who helped to change your life!"

"Right! It was in September, and I was running around con-
stantly on my bike and having a good time. One night I got in
trouble and was put in jail. It wasn't anything really big, but my

uncle came to bail me out. When he saw me, I said, 'Look, I'll pay you back tomorrow morning!' He said, 'No, you won't. My daughter is getting married, and you're going to cut your hair, take a bath, and go to the wedding!'

"Man," I said, "you're putting me on!"

"You're coming to her wedding, or you're going back to jail!"

"I'm going to the wedding then!"

"So I went to the wedding and afterward to the reception. I was sitting at the reception, alone, and wanting to get out of there as fast as I could. Two girls came up to me, and we started talking. I told them who I was, and how the churches were filled with nothing but hypocrites. I shared with them all the venom and hatred I had inside of me, and one of the young ladies pulled out 'The Four Spiritual Laws.' Before she could say anything, I said, 'Hey, I've got one of these!' Hers was all clean, and mine was just filthy. We talked about all this, and she really had that same glow of love and concern that that young man had had. Both these girls seemed to radiate love. So we continued to talk and they told me about a place where everybody loves Jesus, and they wanted to take me there. We went to a Christian coffeehouse.

"I figured that we were going to another place where the Christians were going to 'show off.' They were going to come downtown and save all those lost people down there. So many times I had people come up to me to witness, and it was really false. I had gotten very tired of it, but I said I'd go. We went to a little coffeehouse downtown. We walked in, and the first thing I saw was a man wearing a $200 suit with his arm around a dirty, grimy, young hippy with long hair and no shoes on. The hippy had his arm around the man. Everybody was joined together, and they were thanking Jesus, not for what they had on the outside, but for the happiness they had on the inside. Right then I thought, Man, this is the love that that man had when he witnessed to me.

"Was this the same brand of thing that you had seen in that man's eyes?"

"Right! It was really fantastic because it didn't make any difference whether you were fat or tall, or bald or had long hair, or wore dirty clothes. It didn't make any difference whether you walked up there or whether you drove up in a Caddy. It was what you had in your heart, and they were all happy!"

"Isn't that exciting?"

"They really had life, and abundantly!"

"What did your friend, Madelyn Gandy, do?"

"Well, she got to talking to me, and we were all talking and laughing. I was laughing for the first time in many years. That night I accepted the Lord in my heart. It wasn't an earthshaking prayer I prayed either. I just said, 'Lord, forgive me and if you'll come into my heart, I'll live for you.' Right then I knew I was forgiven."

"George, I remember at this time I got a phone call from these two young ladies saying, "Marge, we want to bring a brand-new Christian down to the college department at church tomorrow.'

"Of course I was thrilled to death, and I remember when they walked in with you. I looked up into your face, the face of a brand-new child of God, and saw such radiance as I've seldom seen in a new Christian. Here was a young man who had lived and done and said and been everything under the sun that we would say was not Christlike, and I saw a most beautiful love shining out of your eyes. And George, I remember how you loved every minute of church, and all the complications of your decision, and the friends you'd left. Share with us about what happened with your friends."

'Well, the boys weren't too pleased about the way I was acting, but they really thought I was sick. They thought I'd dropped some acid and was really out of it. But since then a lot of them have really come to see that I have a love in my heart for them. I want them to know the happiness that I now know. So they're always welcome at my house, and there's always a hot meal. There are plenty of motorcycle parts over there to help them out. I just want them to find what I've found."

"George, I'd like for our readers to know how God's called you to preach and the doors he's opened for you. And how he even gave you a bride-to-be in Madelyn Gandy (remember, she's the girl that he met that night who helped him find this peace and joy) and the joy of falling madly in love."

"Since my salvation, I've been preaching around Houston because I really wanted people to know about how I love the Lord and what he's done for me. There is a little community outside of Houston where they are really on fire. I preached there several times. The pastor, an older man, said he needed some help during the summer and asked me to be associate pastor for that time. I had been praying and asking the Lord to make it possible financially for me to go to college, and sure enough he did that very thing! I was going to earn just enough, not a dollar more, but just enough, to pay my tuition for school for that year."

"George, if you had a message for mothers and dads who feel like the line of communication is completely broken between them and the children, what word of advice would you give them?"

"I'd tell them to expose their children to Christ at an early age, and live Christ before them. Pray for them to feel accepted and loved at home and with friends of their own age."

"George, it really all starts in the home, doesn't it? In working with young people, I find that you have to work with the parents, too. When the line of communication is down, it is very hard to repair, but it can be done through our Lord."

"Marge, if a parent keeps his word, that's a big thing. So many parents tell their children that if they get into trouble to come to them. Then when they do, the parents are embarrassed over what people will think, or they say, 'How could you do this to me?' They should be thinking 'How could you do this to yourself?' "

"Sometimes, as parents, we talk out of both sides of our mouths. We talk a big game, but when the chips are down, we worry about humiliation. We say such things as 'You're killing your mother' or 'You're hurting your father' when the most important thing is what they are doing to their own lives.

"Thank you, George. How I praise God for the beauty of your life now. I know much happiness is in store for you and Madelyn as you serve the Lord together!"

4
Halloween's Over— Take Off That Mask!

Midnight is an interesting time—it could mean almost anything. You may be home sleeping, or if you can't sleep, you may be up reading. Perhaps you are out cruising around town, or maybe just coming home from a date or from work. You may be going over what happened today or thinking about plans for tomorrow.

I was telling some of my friends how much I like the midnight hour, and one of them remarked that this was understandable—it's the "witching hour." I thought about that. Nothing personal, I'm sure.

But for some of us, the dark of the night is the best time for thinking, and perhaps for taking a good look at ourselves. (Some of us may need to do this in the dark of night. There is just so much a body can stand, you know.) At any rate—and in all seriousness— we do need to take a good honest look from time to time and just see what we see.

Often what we come face to face with jars us, and we hide behind some well-known phrases called "rationalization." "Well, that really wasn't my fault—I'm not the president, you know" . . . "Well if I had *her* talent, or *his* capabilities, I'd be quite different" . . . "My family never really understood me; it's their fault I'm the way I am." Or maybe we go a bit further and lay the blame on God: "Well, God made me this way—I just can't help it."

And so on and on, *ad nauseum*. We do it when we're by ourselves, and when we're in front of people. Making excuses has no restricted places or speed limits, unfortunately. It's one of the few manufacturing areas without government control. And everyone's an expert.

But when we take an honest look at ourselves, we realize that all of this simply isn't true. Certainly our backgrounds, experiences, and capabilities *do* color us, but it need not be a case of "color me blah" unless you want it to be.

Sometimes I hear people say, "Under the circumstances, I'm doing the best I can."

And I want to say, "What's a Christian doing *under* the circumstances? You ought to be on top of them!"

Now God is the only one who can hold our hand and help us take an honest look at ourselves, so let's reach out for him right now, and proceed, shall we?

Ready?

All right, let's begin here: What kind of a mask are you wearing?

Instantly you respond, "Hold it, Marge! Surely if I were going to wear a mask, it wouldn't be this one!"

You're hedging again, aren't you? Don't you put on a pious mask when you go to church and a smiling one when you go to parties? Don't you have one mask for work and another for home? Isn't there one for out-of-the-house and one for in-the-house?

We all wear masks, and yet Jesus condemned hypocrisy and role-playing as much as anything in the Bible. And you know something else? I think that's one thing that's turning off so many young people today. They see so much hypocrisy in the adult world.

This was brought home to me in a painful way when my daughter, Gay, was in high school.

My husband, Chuck, and Gay, and I were dressing for Sunday School, and I was supposed to get there early. I had mentioned this several times. But apparently the message had not gotten through because they were laughing and talking and not hurrying like I thought they should. Sure enough, we left late, and I was absolutely livid by the time we drove out. At any rate, I kept thinking how unnecessary all this was, and how thoughtless they

were, and I proceeded to tell them about it all the way to church.
And the more I talked, the worse it got. (Isn't that the way it
usually happens?) Once I got started, I also brought up a few more
things I had not liked in the last few weeks. I blistered their ears.

Well, we pulled up in the church parking lot, and I noticed we
were right beside one of the young girls in my Sunday School class.
I smiled by best smile (such as it is) and said, "Good morning,
Jewel. How are you this bright and sunshiny morning? Isn't it a
beautiful day!"

Behind me I heard a thundering silence. As Jewel went on her
way, I looked around. Gay was studying me very carefully, and
then she remarked in a little voice, "Mother, you can turn it off
and on quicker than anyone I've ever seen."

She made me so mad I thought I'd ground her for a couple of
weeks. But deep down inside, a still small voice was saying, "She's
right, you know."

And she was. It hurt, but she was.

When I ask, What kind of a mask are you wearing? what I am
really asking is, what kind of person are you, and is that the face
you show to the world?

By nature you may be an introvert, you may be an extrovert, or
you may be somewhere in between. That's great—as long as it's you.

You may be the quiet type—a loner. You may like to spend
hours and hours just reading, or listening to music, or doing some
work by yourself—or perhaps just thinking. Well, if this is you,
don't fret because you're not sensational and exciting. You're the
quiet type—and that's wonderful. "Wonderful!" you exclaim in
amazement. "How can that be?"

Stop and think a minute. Remember how Jesus used the quiet
people? It was Andrew—the quiet brother—who found Jesus first
and then shared with his boisterous brother, Peter. God made you
quiet like you are for a purpose just like he did Andrew. Your
job is to find that purpose, not to sit around and sigh because
you're not Peter. Isn't it exciting that in all the world there's not
another like you? There are no two people alike, just like there

are no two identical snowflakes. Even twins have differences.
I've always thought God must have a terrific sense of humor—
just look around you. Aren't we a funny lot most of the time?
Yet God loves us. That's a miracle if I've ever seen one!

That's not you, you say. You're not quiet. You're loud and
boisterous and you crave a lot of attention from people. In fact,
you'd do most anything to get it, like the time you tried to shinny
up the flagpole backwards. You're a real extrovert. Man, that's
great, too. You've got a lot going for you from the beginning. Just
don't ruin it. If you laugh too loud or too long, if you say silly
things just to fill the conversational gap, if you try to be the life of
the party every minute, you'll wear yourself and everybody else
out. You know what I mean? You hear yourself doing it, and you
hate yourself for it. No one would guess how self-conscious you
really are, would they? But let's put down the mask and admit it.
You'd like to be a great person, not a loud one. You really want
to be your best self.

Let me tell you something: That's what God wants you to be
also. Your best self.

Now I can hear you sitting there saying you don't fit into any of
these categories. You're just Miss or Mister In-Between. You've
got a little of this, and a little of that. "Color me nothing—I'm right
in the middle. I'm just a big bore, and I'm bored stiff."

Wait a minute. I'd better color you bright because you have a
bright future. Already you have some balance—a little of this and
a little of that—now all you need is to develop what you have.

That takes in all of us, doesn't it? We're introverts, extroverts, or
in-betweens. And we don't always like what we see in ourselves, so
we wear masks. It's all right for Halloween—I'm back to the "witching hour" again—but it's no deal at all for everyday living!

You want to be you, and I want to be me. Do you believe in
miracles? I do. I've seen miracles happen—lots of them. Christ is
performing them today just as he did long ago when he walked the
earth in human form.

The requirement then was—do you have enough faith?

It's the same today for those who are his children. We can ask him to give us the same radiance he had.

The Bible tells us about the crippled man who sat by the gate called "Beautiful" in Jerusalem. He wasn't just handicapped a little; he was badly crippled from birth. His family and friends took him every day and placed him at the gate, and he begged for everything he had. Can you imagine what it was like to live like that? It wasn't living—it was existing.

Then one day—that started out just like any other—he saw two men walking toward him. Their names were Peter and John. I can just see him now, peering up at them and wondering, Man, are they going to give me any money?

Wonder of all wonders. They stopped and stared at him. And then he heard Peter saying, "Silver and gold have I none; but such as I have, give I thee: In the name of Jesus Christ of Nazareth rise up and walk" (Acts 3:6). And Peter stretched out his hand.

Now notice exactly what happened. Did the man say: "No, sir, I can't do that. You see, I've never walked in my whole life and I certainly can't start now. Why my legs are all shriveled up and knotted, and I'm weak, and . . . and . . ."

Heavens, no! He reached up and took Peter's hand. Then his ankles received strength, and he began leaping for joy.

He didn't ruin a beautiful happening by making excuses. He took a firm grip and acted by faith. And a miracle happened.

It started out just like any other day. And it may do the same thing for you. Jesus may send opportunity in the form of a friend, a telephone call, a note, a book, or perhaps even something we hear on the radio or see on TV. But the door cracks open. A miracle can happen to help you be the person you want to be.

If you want to put aside your mask, let me share with you some guidelines I've found to be helpful through the years.

1. The first thing to do is to *ask Christ to come into your heart and life and to become your Savior.* That's the starting place. He's the author of spiritual sparkle. When I'm physically ill, I want to go to my doctor. He knows me and is interested in me. When you're

in need of spiritual help, who better to go to than the one who made you, and knows you better than you know yourself? Tell him what the problem is; tell him how you feel. You don't have to be a theological giant to talk with God; all you have to do is open up and talk with him right now, right where you are.

2. Now you're in position to *talk with him as his child.* Remember he's anxious to give you good things and to make your life victorious. Jesus put it this way: "I am come that they might have life, and that they might have it more abundantly" (John 10:10).

A good way to begin your talk is to thank him for what he's done and tell him you love him. I know that sometimes Chuck just out of a clear blue sky (he flies a lot) comes in and says, "Marge, I love you so much." And what do I do? I get goose-bumpy all over. It's a thrill to be told something like that out of a clear blue sky— or any sky for that matter. How much our heavenly Father must be pleased when we express our love for him. Thank him for what he's done, tell him you love him, and share your problem with him.

3. *Accept yourself for what you are—a special person.* Stop pounding on the wailing wall because you're not Personality Polly or Beautiful Beulah or Handsome Herman or Warbling Willie. You're you. Take a good look at what you can do and start doing it. If you're a leader, then step out and step up. If you're the shy type, ask the Lord to show you avenues of service where you can really be of help to people. After a while you'll forget all about you, and people won't seem so scarey. If you're the quiet type, seek those pathways seemingly made just for you. They lead to fulfillment for you just as Barbara Bright Lights finds happiness in her world.

The answer, you've noticed, is the same in each instance: Step out with what the Lord has graciously given you.

4. *Respect yourself.* Certainly if you have no self-respect, you can't expect it from others. Of course, I'm not talking about "I" trouble: "I" this, "I" that, "I" something else. I'm talking about the principle the Lord laid down when he said to love your neighbor as yourself. You're a child of the king. All men are your equals—

none any better, none any worse—God made you that way and gave you the power to do great things for him.

Look at the key thoughts here: You're a child of the King, and you have his power to do mighty things. Remembering that it is his power keeps our perspective in place. It's not us. We forget ourselves in doing what he wants done. True humility is not knocking yourself down—it's forgetting yourself.

5. As a Christian, *quit talking about what you don't do.* That may sound strange, but on many campuses I've heard young people who define Christianity in terms of the negative. "Mrs. Caldwell," one freshman said, "I want to introduce myself." She gave me her name, and then added quickly: "Now I want to tell you that I'm a Christian, and I don't drink and I don't dance, I don't take drugs, and I don't use makeup." Right then I thought to myself, Sister, you could use a little. But she was going right on: "I don't . . . and I don't . . . and I don't."

I looked at her and said; "Honey, I don't care what you don't do. Tell me what you are. Tell me what you do; that's the important thing."

It's an old, old story, but like many ancient tales, it's still true: what you are speaks so loud I can't hear what you say. If you stand for something, you don't run the danger of falling for nothing.

Well, that's it. These are the five guidelines, the quintet of suggestions that can make the real you blossom forth. Do you think it's worth trying? Are you tired of a ho-hum existence, plain boredom, or perhaps that ever-present gnawing deep inside you that says you're still goofing?

Things can be different for you as they were for the lame man . . . "In the name of Jesus Christ of Nazareth . . ."

"Get up and walk" can refer to far more than the physical.

It did for Sharon—or at least I'll call her that. I had gone to Arizona as a modeling and charm teacher some years ago. My daughter went with me; it was to be for six weeks. On the day camp started, I met my first modeling class, and they were many in number. (It was not my popularity, the course was required.)

Among my teenagers was Sharon.

Well, she glared at me and stomped around, dressed in tight blue jeans and a dirty shirt. She couldn't care less about modeling. You had to be all wet or four-legged to get along with Sharon; swimming and horses were all she cared about. Add to this the fact that she was twenty pounds overweight, had bushy eyebrows, and wore her hair in a stiff ponytail (horses again), and you have a portrait of Sharon, a picture of rebellion.

I started the usual place. "Sharon, stand straight. Let me see how you look."

"I'm standing straight as I can, and I don't want to take this old course anyway."

That makes two of us, I thought. If I could get this girl to change, I deserve a medal. Then I noticed something else. Each day the girls would tell me how Sharon would argue about religion with just anyone and everyone. She claimed to be an agnostic, said there wasn't really a God, and laughed in the face of those who believed. She succeeded in thoroughly confusing several girls.

One lovely evening after vespers, she approached me. "Mrs. Caldwell, I want to talk to you about religion."

"No, Sharon," I replied. "I don't argue about religion. I know God's not dead. I love Christ with all my heart, and I really don't want to argue with you about it."

"I don't want to argue" was her surprising retort, "but there are some things I really want to know."

I decided I'd find out if she was serious by making it hard for her.

"Well, Sharon," I said, "I'm a counselor in a cabin, and I don't have a lot of extra time. If you really want to talk about it, I'll be glad to. Let's meet at five-thirty in the morning on the porch of my cabin. Okay?"

"That's a deal," she called back over her shoulder and ran off to the canteen.

My soul and body! What in the world had I done? Five-thirty in the morning! I must be out of my mind! I'm eating breakfast at seven-thirty, but I'm not awake.

However, I set my alarm, and before I could get dressed the next morning, there she was. We went out into that indescribably beautiful Arizona morning, crisp and cool and quiet, and sat under a small mesquite tree. We began by just talking, and all of her questions tumbled out. Finally, about an hour and a half later, I opened my Bible and showed her how to become a Christian. She accepted Christ right there. Her prayer asking him to come into her heart and life was one of the most halting, yet precious prayers I'd ever heard. And then I thanked him for coming into her life.

As we began to leave, I said, "Happy Birthday, Sharon. This is your birthday, you've been born again today." Large tears began to roll down that girl's cheeks, and she asked if she might tell the camp director what had happened to her that morning.

How thrilled we all were at the change that immediately began to take place in Sharon's life. First, she apologized to most of the girls for her rude and discourteous attitudes, and then she came and asked me for a Bible. We got her one, and marked some Scriptures for her.

One day in modeling class she said, "Mrs. Caldwell, I really want to learn to model, and don't you think something should be done about my eyebrows and my hair?"

I was so excited. Immediately I put her on a diet. Then we practically sat on her and plucked her eyebrows. Next, we cut her hair in a fashionable style and taught her about the styles that would be most flattering to her figure.

As the weeks passed, Sharon became the subject of conversation. She learned to model quickly because she wanted to learn. She quit slumping. She began to memorize Scripture passages and came back often for me to mark more for her. She started to laugh a lot and to tease. In a very short time, she won all the girls over as friends. I have never seen a girl so happy. She changed before our very eyes.

But, listen, the real change came on the inside first, and then we began to see the results on the outside. That's the way it works.

The last day of camp, we were all boarding the train for home, and I was on the same train with Sharon as we traveled back to Texas. Suddenly, she asked, "Will you get off the train when we get to my hometown and meet my family?"

"Sure," I said. "What time do we get there?"

"Three-thirty in the morning," she said.

Three-thirty in the morning! But of course I wanted to meet her family and was anxious to see them when they saw the new Sharon.

When we stepped off the train, there they were. Her mother and her father and her brother were looking at her so eagerly, and she hugged them all and then turned and introduced me. We talked a minute, and then she asked. "Mother, do you see anything different about me?"

"Well, honey, your hair is cut and your eyebrows—where are they? Why, Sharon, you've lost weight. You look great."

"But don't you notice something else?" she persisted.

"Let's see now. Yes, there is something, but I can't put my finger on it. Your eyes seem different . . . yes, honey, there is something."

"Mother," Sharon explained, "You sent me off to camp to get finished, but I've just gotten started. I'm a Christian now, and I'm happier than I've ever been in my life. Mother, it's wonderful!"

I told them good-bye and cheerfully hugged Sharon. As I lay in my bunk that night, I thanked God for the inner radiance that he had given to a young girl at camp. Before my very eyes I had seen a physical change come over her as the result of a thrilling change that had taken place in her heart.

Is change possible? Yes indeed. But the change that comes only on the outside is temporary because we do it all ourselves. It's mostly talk. But the change that comes on the inside is from God, and it can only be caught. When Christ touches our lives with a spark from above, it happens this way. Change is inevitable.

And you know what? It all starts with you. And with all this at your fingertips, you just can't afford not to be you, can you?

Throw away that mask!

Halloween's over!

You're on your way!

5
Mothers Have Eyes in the Back of Their Head

Have you ever wondered how in the world your mother knew so
much? How did she know all those things unless she really *did* have
eyes in the back of her head! When I was quite young I wouldn't
dare talk back to my mother, but oh, how mad I'd get! One day I
decided to just stick my tongue out at her! Now, I was standing
in my room at just the right angle to be seen in the mirror, but I had
my back toward her! She said:

"Marjorie, I saw you stick your tongue out at me!"

How in the world did she know? When I asked her, she answered,

"I always know everything you do!"

She really convinced me that she did know what I did no matter
where I was! For years I'd come home and tell her what I'd done
that I shouldn't have. The way I saw it, I might as well tell her because she'd know anyway!

I can remember these sayings of hers so well!

"Take your raincoat, it's going to rain today!"

And you know what? It rained! Mothers just *know!*

"If you iron that dress with a very hot iron, it'll ruin the fabric!"

And you know what? It ruined it! Mothers just *know!*

"If you let Jim know you're crazy about him, he'll lose interest!"

Yes! You guessed it! I did, 'n he did! How do mothers know
everything?

"If you buy the Levis too tight, you won't be able to wear them
after they're laundered!"

How does my mother know all this?

Many years ago (about 100 I think, 'n that's a joke!) when I was a teenager, Mother would say, "Pretty is as pretty does!"

I would get so mad! And then she'd come out with, "Marge, be *so* careful what you do, because there's always someone watching you!"

That would make me mad, too! I'd frown and say, "Then let them watch somebody else, because I'm tired of being watched."

I'd often wonder how in the world mothers know so much. And it made me feel very uncomfortable lots of times when I'd know without a doubt that Mother could read between the lines. When I'd start rationalizing with Daddy about a broken rule in the house, I'd glance over at Mother and she'd have that look on her face that said very plainly "I know better!"

There are those times when you're blue, depressed, and you don't know what's wrong! You don't know to whom to go, or where to turn. You just throw yourself across your bed and start to cry! Mother slips in and sits on the side of the bed and starts rubbing your back. She doesn't say a word—just sits there and lets the warmth of her love flow over to you! Could she *possibly* understand? Could there be *any* way she could know the hurt a young girl feels when her boyfriend has left for good?

Yes, for she had that same experience when she was young! She's sitting there rubbing your back and thinking aloud about another girl years ago who was also alone and blue, depressed, and with a broken heart! How she *yearned* for someone! But there was no one. She can remember thinking to herself, If I ever have a daughter . . . when she needs me I'm going to be there . . . loving, understanding, and sympathetic!"

Then there was the time you had your first date (with the boy your parents didn't like), remember?

"What don't you like about him, Mother?" you asked.

"I don't *know!* I can't put my finger on *why!* I'm just afraid if you go out with him, you'll have to fight him off all night! Honey, I just know!" she answered.

"Well, if that isn't the most unfair thing I've ever heard you say!"

you snapped!

And so it went! You went on the date. Think back! Remember at the hamburger drive-in? He kept talking about the parking and the making out you'd do—and you were absolutely panicky! You felt trapped! A still, small voice kept saying, "Mother was *right!* It's going to be weird! And what if I just can't handle him?"

Just in the nick of time, just when your date was getting ready to drive off, here comes Mother speeding up! You thought for a moment she was going to drive through the drive-in! She rolled down the window and shouted:

"Honey, I've been trying to locate you! Your grandmother will be arriving tonight in about an hour, and I knew you'd want to go to the airport! She'd *die* if you weren't there! I'm *so* sorry to interrupt your date! Jim, could you please forgive us if we borrow your date? It's *really* important that she be with us!"

Oh! How humiliated you acted! Imagine! Your first date! And your parents looking for you . . . and worse . . . *finding* you! After you're safe in your car, you ask: "Mother, I thought Grandmother was coming tomorrow night!" "She is! I just thought maybe you would like to see me tonight, so I came to help!"

In the darkness of the car you smiled! You felt warm and safe, loved and protected all at the same time! Who tells mothers what's going on and when you need them the most?

Remember when you were thirteen? One night your folks were having a college fellowship at your house. All the students were singing and laughing. Then they started giving their testimonies as to how God was working in their lives. They shared their joys, doubts, feelings of guilt . . . their frustrations! You were listening in the doorway. Then you began to think of your own life: how you neglected to share Christ at school, how you hid behind all kinds of excuses, then the devil really hit you in the pit of your stomach!

"If you were saved," he kept saying to you, "you wouldn't feel like this. If you really knew Jesus, you'd be turned on, not a weakling like you are now!"

After a few minutes, you turned and slipped upstairs! Tears were about to come, so you quietly closed the door, threw yourself on your bed, and began to sob!

Here came the devil again! He asked: "If you were saved, how could you have the thoughts you do—or not love God more than you do?"

Someone's at your door! You get very still as your door slowly opens—Mother slips in quietly! She doesn't say a word for awhile! Then she starts telling the story of *her* spiritual life as a teenager. She shares with you a large segment of her home and church life— her doubts, her fears! You can't believe your ears! She's telling you how she doubted her salvation and how guilty she felt until she remembered how great God is to forgive and start over with you! She shared how she'd promised God that she would always love and help young people because she understood how they felt!

She was in your room almost an hour! Then she leaned over and kissed you on the cheek. You heard her asking Jesus to hold you close and help you to bring your doubts and fears to him. Then she was gone, and you wondered if you'd dreamed all this! No! She was there alright! You feel so grateful! How do mothers just know when you need them the most?

Remember the time you had a slumber party for your friends? Oh, were you excited! You planned for weeks and weeks and changed the menu for the midnight snack at least seven times! You cleaned house Friday afternoon until it was spotless! (Next time you'd wait until after the slumber party to clean!) Then the day finally arrived, and so did your friends!

Mother brought out trays and trays of food. After cases of Cokes, everybody laughed and played games and shared little things you always share at slumber parties. What fun! Then remember when the boys drove up uninvited and how secretly thrilled you were? Remember how they came on in with their beer, and you nearly *died!* What would your folks do? What kind of scene would they make? It'd be all over school next week about how square you and your folks were! How could you face everybody? What would your friends think?

Then your dad came in! He smiled and in a very courteous, firm way asked the boys to leave. They did leave, and you felt your face getting hot! Oh, you were so embarrassed!

The girls thanked your dad, and to your utter amazement, told you how lucky you were to have such great folks who were firm, but not ugly with the boys!

"You know where you stand with your dad," they said, "and you know he means what he says! Gosh! It must be great to have folks like yours!"

You felt so proud! Yet you felt a little guilty because of your lack of trust in your parents' judgment. Aren't parents something else?

Honestly, though, when you look at it that way, the old generation gap isn't so wide after all! It really came as a jolt to me to realize that my parents had gone through many of the heartaches, disappointments, and trials that I was going through. It really shook me up when I realized that all they wanted for me was happiness, and they wanted to shield me from the mistakes they'd made. When I began to understand, my parents began to be *people*—not just parents! Look at your folks! Don't they do the funniest things? I'll bet it's because they love you so much! What do you think?

I got to thinking about discipline! How I hated that part of growing up! I didn't realize that discipline was a facet of love, that it would be much easier on my folks if they just let me go on and didn't reprimand me! When they'd discipline me by taking the phone and car away from me, I'd just wish they'd go to the movie or somewhere so I could call my current boyfriend and tell him why I couldn't talk to him that night! But do you think they'd stir from the house? Heavens no! And I'd get furious! Now I know that to "stick to their guns" meant inconveniencing them, too!

How I used to scream (as much as I thought I could get away with!) over how unfair they were! One day my Mother laughed and said:

"Marge, I hope I'm around when you have a teenage daughter, and she thinks you're so unfair and so old-fashioned!"

I thought to myself, Well, I can tell you one thing! I'm not going to be like this with her if I do have a daughter!

One day when our daughter, Gay, was fifteen and we were living in West Texas, Mother was visiting us. Gay came in and asked, "Mother, can I go with the gang to the movie?" She was dressed in cutoffs and a tiny shirt that would make a bikini look sick!

"You may go to the movie . . . but not until you put on some other outfit!" I replied.

"Mother! *Everybody's* dressed like this! I'll feel so stupid!"

"I don't care what *everybody's* dressed like, I just care what *you* look like!"

She bristled, "Mother, you are *so* old-fashioned!"

I heard this muffled laughter, and I looked over my shoulder. My mother was practically rolling on the floor with hysteria! She was laughing so hard by then that even Gay looked aghast!

"What's wrong with Grandmother?" she asked.

"Oh, nothing!" I replied, as I glared at my mother.

"My prayers are answered!" she laughed, "but Gay, you wouldn't understand! But your mother does!"

If you're lucky enough to still have your mother with you, why don't you do something? When you finish reading this, go look her up, or call her, and tell her how much you love her! Now, when she recuperates from this shock, she'll be so excited, and so will you! Ask God to help you understand your mom. Pray for her daily, and watch the changes, they'll be in *both* of you! It's like a miracle! I'm excited about what's going to happen in your house!

6
The Merry-go-round Called Love

"Love is what makes the world go round—in a very merry way."

I think I must have thought of the idea of love and merry-go-rounds a long time before the songwriters did. Maybe it's because of my first true love. He was five and very handsome; I was four and very there. He used to ride a big, white horse and would stand high in the saddle trying to catch the gold ring that made its appearance every now and then as a special challenge to the riders. Of course, I was right behind him trying to land him and the gold ring also. I never did, but I came close the time I got a brass ring instead. The only problem was that it was attached to a lady's hat, which made for a rather difficult situation.

But that was a year or two ago. And looking back now from the broad base of the middle years (in every sense), I'd have to say that what I thought then was right: "Love is what makes the world go round in a very merry way."

In all seriousness, love is very important in the life of any individual, no matter what your age might be. I think, however, this is especially true of the teenage years and through the early twenties. The influence of our "love life" permeates all of our thinking. It is during this time that we are doing our serious dating, that we're looking for someone—that certain someone—with whom we will be spending the rest of our lives. It's exciting; it's traumatic; it's important. The boy-girl game is as old as the hills and as new as tomorrow. I use the word "game" because in a certain sense there's a lot of this in it. It's a challenge. "How can I catch him?" "How can I get her attention?" It's part of the fun. In many ways it's a good part; by this process we get to know people better, and thus come to realize more of what we're looking for or what we hope to find in a life mate.

So much of the counseling that Chuck and I have done in the past several years has pertained to boy-girl relationships, man-woman relationships before marriage and after marriage. Through it all, there are some things that keep popping up over and over again like bread in an automatic toaster. And like some toast, they are "burned to a crisp." The automatic factor was working, but it follows the guidelines of God's laws, not man's desires—if these two are in conflict.

Many areas here are subjects for wide and deep discussion. Let's touch on a few: dating—and who has the hardest time getting started; the love-sex bit (If this is a bit, I hope I never see a mountain!); the case of one-sided love; and some guidelines for selecting a life partner.

Starting at the beginning (always a good place to start)—who has it harder, the girl or the boy?

"You know, Mrs. Caldwell, it's awful. I have to just sit around and wait for him to ask me and hope that he does. The boys sure have the best end of the deal because they can take the initiative and ask for dates, and so on."

And then there comes the letter which says: "I wonder if you know how it feels to get your courage up to ask a girl for a date, to wait for the right time and the right moment—and then have her turn you down flat. It isn't just the no, it just seems to do something to your ego, to your pride."

And so, like many other things, there are two sides to the story Nowadays, however, the figures seem to get kind of blurred. It seems that today some girls feel that there are no lines drawn and think nothing of starting the whole thing, of initiating the dating situation. Maybe my words are truer spoken than I realized. "Think nothing" is probably rather accurate. That's what happens in that situation. The girl really isn't thinking, because most boys run from a girl who does the chasing. It just doesn't work. You'll lose a boy much faster by chasing after him.

"Oh," but you say, "you're just not with it, Mrs. Caldwell. The sexual revolution is here and things are different."

Yes, some do say that we're in a sexual revolution. I imagine that's rather accurate. It's sex, not love. Love is many parts. Sex is just one part of love, and it's wonderful. When I say "I like sex" in some high school or college meeting, I can see the teenagers looking at me in amazement.

"My soul! How can you? You're too old!" they're thinking.

But sex is absolutely wonderful, under the right circumstances. Why shouldn't it be? God thought it up. He's not up there perched on a fuzzy little cloud pointing a bony finger down at us and saying: "Naughty, Naughty! Don't do this! Mustn't do that!"

God is the author of love. But because we are human beings and need guidance and help, he provides both. Sex is from God, and given to operate within a certain structure. It is one part of love, not love itself.

But in our day and age, society has put the word sex up in neon lights, both literally and figuratively, so that many young people have come to equate sex with love. They're not equal, anymore than the icing equals the cake. One is a part of the other, but just a part.

In that sense there is a sexual revolution, but that's just it. It's sex, not love. Underneath, people are still people like they were in the days of Moses. They love and they hate. They are jealous, envious, happy, sad, selfish, unselfish—just people. Human nature hasn't altered a bit.

Some of the lines being handed out today are the same ones that Noah must have used to tie up the ark. There are still boys who say, "If you love me, you will . . ."

That's not love in any sense of the word.

Love is unselfish; love is wanting the best good of the beloved, and certainly a boy who asks a girl to surrender her morality and her standards is not thinking of her good.

A similar approach is the one in which the words "I love you" are used in an effort to achieve the desired results. But here the pronouns are mixed up. What he ought to be saying is "I love me" because that's the person he's thinking about.

On the other side of the picture (and neither side is very attractive) is the girl who lures a boy on and then complains that he "went on the make." There's nothing new about luring either. Delilah tried it a long time ago on Samson and brought about the first crew cut in history. But at least she didn't complain about the situation later.

Whatever approaches, what "reasoning," whatever hogwash is handed out, fornication is still wrong. (That's a big word meaning sex before marriage.) No one is a winner. Yes, I know everyone wants to do his own thing, "to do what comes naturally." If you followed this line of thought, you'd be hitting someone in the head every time you got mad.

Traditionally, the girls are the losers, but it can work havoc in the life of a young man as well.

Today's young people sometimes enter into what they call a "meaningful relationship." The relationship has meaning all right, but not the kind they think it does.

I am remembering a young man in one of our Texas colleges who came to me to discuss another problem. In our conversation, however, it developed that he and his girl friend had set up housekeeping together, without benefit of marriage. Each thought the circumstances to be ideal. "We want to be bound together by our love for each other," he told me, "and not because somebody stood in front of us and went through a ritual. We think this is the truest kind of love; there are no shackles."

It was not quite a year later when he sat in the same room, deeply despondent, tremendously hurt, and told me with a voice that came close to breaking; "I can look back now and see where I made my mistake, Mrs. Caldwell. I should have asked her to marry me. You see, if she had some kind of security, some kind of social structure to hang on to, she might not have walked out on me. I always heard it was the woman who pays, but I don't think it worked out that way in this case."

You don't break God's laws. They break you.

But let's look for a while at the other side. Let's think about the fun part, the exciting part, the bright lights and happy part. The dating game is never going out of style. It's so important to see him or to see her—this person in whom you are interested—in as many different circumstances as possible. We're all on our good behavior on dates, but what about at home, at school, at work? It's good to be alone with him or with her, but it's also good for the two of you to be with others and see how he or she relates to other people. There need to be times when you do things together. There need to be times when you just sit and talk. I guess this would be where you'd step off the merry-go-round and just sort of sit and be. Then, as things become more serious, perhaps you need to do a little adding, and this may lead to a little subtracting also. There are nine questions that should be considered. You need to be able to answer at least six with a "yes." Ideally, your "yes's" would be more than that, and if they are, you're really doing okay!

Here are the questions

1. Do you have similar religious beliefs? Of course to share the same religious beliefs and to belong to the same church also is the ideal situation, but we don't always have the ideal.

Your religious beliefs, however, do need to be similar. And you need to decide before marriage which church you will attend. All too often "I'll go to mine and he will go to his" works out that neither goes to neither.

Yes, I know that all persons within a denomination do not believe alike. Nor do we all believe alike within a given church. But the important thing is that you must have similar religious beliefs and you must decide before marriage which church to attend.

2. Do you have similar family backgrounds economically? If one of you comes from a well-to-do-family (the servant bit and all that) and the other has to hold the nickles until the buffalo grows a beard, there may be some difficulty in this area.

3. Do you come from similar backgrounds socially? While it is true that our towns are no longer so sharply divided as to "right side" of the tracks and "wrong side," still the people with whom you grew up, your family, your friends, and their friends have made a decided impression upon you. They have molded many of your patterns of thinking and behaving, whether you realize it or not.

4. Do you like the same activities? Or, if not, do you have an appreciation for the activities that your loved one enjoys? Girls, you may not be a golfer. Boys, you may think that any antique shop is just another word for an old folks home. But if your loved one is gung ho on a certain activity or hobby, do you share that enthusiasm? If not, can you be understanding about his enjoying it?

5. Do you have similar educational backgrounds? Notice here also that the word used is "similar," not "identical." Of course, many marriages have survived without this, but it's also been the point at which several were broken. One of the saddest things is to hear a couple say, "We just don't have anything to talk about anymore."

I remember an instance when friends of mine graduated from high school and wanted to get married. The plan was that she put him through college and then it would be her turn. However, when he finished college he wanted to become a teacher, and so he furthered his education. She was in favor of this also, and continued her secretarial work begun shortly after graduating from high school. I remember her saying one time just before he got his PhD: "We just don't seem to have anything to say to each other. He's gone so far, I just don't know how to talk with him."

They drifted apart and ultimately were divorced. It wasn't necessarily anyone's fault, but it happened. Similar educational backgrounds is a decided asset.

6. Do you have the same desire for children? You'd think that everybody talks about this ahead of time, but they don't. Do you want children? Does your prospective mate? Are you thinking in terms of a small family or a large one? Do you plan to wait a while

after marriage for them, or do you plan to have your family immediately?

7. Do both of you plan to work and, if so, how do you plan to divide the housework? I am thinking of two young friends of mine who started off to college both having been honor graduates in high school. The girl was commenting that both of them planned to work, and I asked, "Well, who's going to do the cooking?"

"I am," she replied.

"What about the dishwashing?"

"Me," she answered.

"Well, what about the clothes and the housecleaning?"

"I'm going to do it." she replied.

I looked at her a little bit startled and said, "Well, if both of you are working, wouldn't it follow that perhaps both of you would help out around the house?"

She shook her head: "Nope. He's worth it. He shouldn't ever have to come home and fool with that kind of thing. I'll do it."

So off they went to school and to their respective jobs. After a while, she began to have that feeling on the inside that she had the short end of the stick, that he wasn't carrying his share of the load. She really hadn't thought her way through it in the beginning. She loved him, she wanted to make things right and easy for him, but they hadn't really gotten down to the nitty-gritty of it all.

Who is going to do the dishes when both of you work?

8. Does the husband-to-be have a respectable vocation? Now I don't mean is he a bank president. I'm asking if whatever he does is respectable. Can you be proud of him in his job?

9. And then, are the two of you old enough to be emotionally mature? Of course, the term "emotional maturity" is loaded and could go off in any direction. I am speaking of persons who have reached such a level of emotional stability that the close relationship of marriage will stand the strain. It should not be a roller-coaster existence of ups and downs because of childishness, unwarranted jealousy, feelings worn on the sleeve, etc. (Incidentally,

this is one style that never seems to change. There are always those among us who wear their feelings on their sleeve.)

This is a list well worth mulling over some long winter's evening while you have your hot Dr. Pepper with lemon slices. Add up your answers. Can you come up with at least six "yes's"? If not, as I mentioned earlier, you may need to do a little subtracting.

Yes, you may need to "subtract" yourself from the situation, or you may find that someone else has done it for you. That's the kind that can hurt.

"But he said he loved me, Mrs. Caldwell, and now he's dating other people and I have to go and sit by him in class or I pass him on the campus or we have the same time for coffee break in our building or something, and it just hurts. I just don't understand."

Yes, it does hurt and at this point on the merry-go-round you feel like you have missed the gold ring in every sense of the word. But let's stop and look at the situation.

"He said he loved me." Really, it would appear that he didn't because if he did, then he wouldn't be leaving you for someone else. We use the term "I love you" so glibly. Does it mean you care for someone else above all others? Does it mean you care for that person more than you care for yourself?

When you've had to subtract someone or you have been subtracted, life is not over, though you may feel at the moment that it is. (No, the bills will still be coming in at the first of the month.) It is true that sometimes you feel at this point that no one really cares about you, that no one gives a flip whether you come or go or whether you don't.

No one cares? Someone does. Jesus does. He cares so much that it hurts. My first suggestion would be for you to get to know him. Recently I had the most wonderful experience. I was talking with a young woman and she said she had heard about the Bible but she had never had one. I had the privilege of buying one for her.

Read its pages. Get to know him or talk to someone who does. And find out that there has been a Person, there is a Person, who loved you enough to die for you. He also said, "I am come that they might have life, and that they might have it more abundantly" (John 10:10). That's exactly what he meant.

"Oh," but you say, "I don't want to go to him. I don't want to bother him with my little tiny details, all the nitty-gritty stuff, not something like that. It's just—you know—I don't want to bother him."

But he wants you to. He loves you and he's told you that even the hairs on your head are all numbered. He said that not even a sparrow falls but what he knows it. All the little things, as well as all the big things, he wants to take care of in your life. He wants to lift the burden.

Right now you hurt. Talk to him about it. Just you and the Lord. Turn it all over to him, and ask him to take away that hurt in your heart and to give you a peace. And you know what? He'll do it.

It may not happen in a day or a week, and you may have to go on sitting next to that certain guy in class, or seeing her at coffee break, but there'll come a time when you'll notice that the hurt's gone. There's a new kind of a peace in your heart, a sort of feeling that all is well with the world.

And sometimes there comes a moment later when you'll look at him and think, What did I ever see in him? Or maybe, What was there about her that I liked anyway?

You know what else? God has something great for you. The Bible says: "Trust in the Lord with all thine heart; and lean not on thine own understanding" (Prov. 3:5). I don't know what it is, but the Lord knows. I don't know who it is the Lord has in mind for you, but he knows.

The Bible also says: "In all thy ways acknowledge him, and he shall direct thy paths" (Prov. 3:6). And suddenly one day—or perhaps gradually—there'll come into your life a new someone and things will all be different.

One-sided love is about as much fun as a toothache when the dentist is out of town. But there is Someone who can take care of the situation, and one day you'll notice the sun is shining again. Perhaps you'll even want to take a little walk in the late summer evening over to the vacant lot where the band parents are staging the annual carnival. There you'll see the merry-go-round, and you'll think: Love is like that. It's a merry-go-round.

If you do, hop on. When the right hour strikes on God's time piece, you'll catch the gold ring if you're supposed to. When you do, I hope for your sake it's not attached to anyone's hat.

7
Romance—the Married Kind

What do you think of when I say "romance"?

One teenager responded instantly: "Oh joy, oh bliss, oh hot-buttered toast!" (And her figure reflected it.)

Your concept may be a little different. When I say "romance," you may drift off on cloud nine (which is a little crowded by this time) and muse: "He is tall, dark, handsome, and his car is out of this world!"

Or, if you're a male-type person, you may get that certain look (not to be confused with indigestion) and reflect almost to yourself: "She is something else! She's about average height, has blond hair, and sort of blue-green eyes, and is stacked like you wouldn't believe!"

Or—if you're a little older—perhaps you would think of a place. The eyes of your heart may suddenly see Acapulco with its unbelievably blue water or the sun-drenched beaches of Waikiki—you may think of the indescribable splendor of the Grand Canyon (forgetting, of course, the mule ride down the Canyon) or perhaps Niagara Falls. (I kept thinking to myself, "Surely they turn this thing off at night!")

But whatever the word means to you, romance can be a very lovely time of life, and it can be made to last a lifetime. Romance can build; it can tear down. Like most relationships, it has certain elements which can help to make for success if recognized and applied. Of course the approach, the method that each of us would use would be different. Let's talk about romance—the married kind.

I am rembering just now a letter I received from a Houston
housewife. It went something like this:

Dear Mrs. Caldwell:

I really have no specific gripe, but something is wrong, and
I don't know exactly what it is.

Let me describe my marriage and my family.

I'm married to a wonderful man, who is thirty-five. I am
thirty-two. He's neat and nice-looking. I'm not pretty, but
in my better days, I was told I was quite neat and attractive.
I had a nice figure, and seemingly nice hair—I kept getting com-
pliments on it.

We have three children whose ages are two, seven, and nine.

I've always prided myself on being what my husband wanted
and needed; we've been married eleven years. He's very successful, and we have all we need and want.

Really, I feel ashamed that I'm complaining. Maybe I have
a sixth sense or something, but when I heard your "Speak Out
with Marge" program over Station KXYZ the other night, you
mentioned that sometimes romance goes out of a marriage,
communication breaks down, and trouble begins. That's
what's happening to us, and I'm really scared. My husband
and I seem to be poles apart. Our only conversation is about
our kids' problems or painting the house or going to the
PTA, or something like that.

I'll admit I don't give him much time, but with three
kids . . . ?

Can you give me any suggestions?

The letter was signed by a Houston housewife. Let's call
her "Mrs. G."

I appreciated this letter. I was grateful for her frankness, which
always assists us in trying to be helpful. I attempted to put myself
in her shoes (considering the size of my feet, I am confident this
was wishful thinking) and to remember what it felt like to be on the
other side of the fence, asking for advice.

Sometimes I have been on the other side. It seems like I'm either on one side or the other, but never in the middle. (I get caught in the middle many times, but that's another story.) At any rate, I am frequently without the facts, but naturally this doesn't stop me from having strong and vocal opinions.

When I am on the "asking" side, I don't want someone to treat my problem lightly or to give me some nebulous or intangible advice that I can't translate into everyday living. I want them to let me have it one, two, three. That I can use.

And since I have always wanted specific help, I thought perhaps this lady would also.

Mrs. G. said in her letter, "In my better days . . . I had a nice figure . . . I always prided myself . . ."

And that reminded me of a story, a true story, that happened to me. I should say it happened to Chuck and me and to our family life.

As I have mentioned, my husband is in the oil business, and when this happened we had been transferred to Houston from Oklahoma City. I suppose we had only been in south Texas a few weeks. As I remember, I was thirty-fivish, or something like that. (That was three years before I got to be thirty-eight, where I have been ever since.)

At this point in our lives together, I was wondering if all the romance hadn't gone out of our marriage. It seemed to me that Chuck just wasn't as attentive as he used to be. True, he was trying to get ahead in business and working hard to be the "ace salesman" of his company, but after all—there was still "l'il ole me!"

We had two little school-age children, and I was so tired of making peanut butter and jelly sandwiches I thought I'd just turn into one—that would catch his attention.

Well, I had sort of let myself go. I remember I spent most of my time in an old housecoat which had two or three buttons off and the hem half out, but it was comfortable. It was my "security blanket."

I'd put it on early in the morning, and slip into some old slides I had, and put my hair up. That was before the days of rollers; we used bobby pins. So I had these curls all over my head with the pins sticking out sideways—something like a disgruntled porcupine. With no makeup on, I'm sure I looked rather sickly, like I was just recovering from yellow jaundice.

Anyway, that was the way I looked in the morning when I went in to fix breakfast and lunches for the kids.

You know there are some things that none of the books tell you. Nowhere do you find any information on the adjustment required for two people to get up at the same time every morning.

Chuck is one of those nauseating men who gets up bright and early. He's as alert at 5:30 in the morning (I think he is; I really can't see too well) as he is at that same hour in the evening. He moves cheerily about and sings in the shower and loves everyone, and I could just die.

When I get up in the morning, I have to sit on the side of the bed and think about it for a few minutes. I just can't jump up bright and shiny.

So that's the way it was every morning. I'd fumble my way into the kitchen to make those everlasting peanut butter sandwiches, fix breakfast, and get everything going. Chuck would come sailing in bubbling with cheerfulness.

"Honey, have my shirts come home yet?"

I'd just look at him and want to say, "They haven't even gone out yet," but, of course, I'd never give myself away like that. Anyway, he'd lean over to kiss me, and I'd turn my cheek, and after breakfast he was gone. The last thing he'd hear as he went out the door was: "I haven't got this . . . and you didn't do that . . . and why can't you ever fix anything . . . and there's no carpet in the living room . . . *ad nauseum.* I really felt sorry for myself.

But all that changed one day. Chuck came in and said, "Marge, I want you to dress up real pretty today, and come down and meet my new secretary. I told him I would. I had visions of his new secretary: about a size twenty-two, the matronly type, always taking care of him.

This was my thinking when I fixed myself up to look my best and went downtown to give the old girl a thrill. I did the best with what

I had to work with and went to the office.

WHAMMY! DOUBLE WHAMMY!!

I have never been so sick in all my life. Chuck did introduce me to his new secretary—obviously a fugitive from a Miss America contest. She was a size ten, and absolutely sickening.

The whole thing made me furious. She'd lean over to pour his coffee and murmur, "May I pour you some more coffee, Mr. Caldwell?"

I wanted to say: "Let him pour his own coffee. He does at home."

I was fit to be tied. When I get that mad at Chuck, the only thing I know to do is go downtown and spend some of his money. I did. I went straight down to an exclusive shop and bought a beautiful new housecoat with some slippers to match, and I went home. I was going to get so dressed up the next day he couldn't stand it.

I set the alarm for thirty minutes earlier the next morning and got up, splashed cold water on my face to wake up (ugh), put on my new clothes, fixed my makeup, rolled up my hair long enough to fix it also, and was in the kitchen when Chuck came whistling down the hall.

He stopped in the doorway. There was a sort of gasping noise.

Then he called out: "Hey, kids, come in here! I don't know where your Mother is, but there's the sexiest looking doll in the kitchen you ever saw!"

Later Chuck told me: "Marge, you just don't know how much I wanted you to dress up and look nice in the morning. I know it's hard with two kids and all you have to do, but . . . ."

That gave me a warm glow, and I knew it was well worth it all. I remembered the previous mental picture he had of me when he left—looking like I did—griping about everything. And then I thought of that sweet young thing at the office with her revolting "May I pour you some more coffee, Mr. Caldwell." I knew I'd better watch out—and take a second look at myself.

It's a long story, but it makes an important point. One of the first things we need to do when we feel the romance has gone out of our marriage is to take an honest look at ourselves.

Go in the bathroom or the bedroom, or wherever you have a full-length mirror, and take a good look. It may make you feel not-so-good. Incidentally, if you don't have a full-length mirror, please get one. You can hide a multitude of sins without it.

Mrs. G. said that in her better days, she had a good figure. She could have one again; so could you. True, it takes work, but then most worthwhile things do. Look upon it as an investment, and it's one which will likely pay rich dividends.

When you have little children, it takes quite a bit of effort to keep yourself lovely, especially in the morning. But remember you don't have to be beautiful, or most of us would be up a creek without a paddle. You can keep yourself neat. Your hair can be combed, and lipstick takes just a minute if you don't have time for a complete makeup job.

I know a young lady in Houston. (Young? She's thirty-eight!) She's a model and just lovely. Even with all that built-in advantage, she keeps a neat housecoat handy she can jump into each morning, one that is long and lovely, and puts on her lipstick and combs her hair. She tells me it just takes a little time, and it's certainly the smart thing to do. It pays off for her; it can for you also.

Incidentally, there's the "coming home" time that's important also, where both children and husband are concerned. I remember a little thirteen-year-old girl who commented, "My mother's always telling me to stand up, hold my shoulders back, get the spot off my dress, and all that stuff. But when I come home from school, she's still in the same old dumb housecoat she had on in the morning."

There's a point there for us mothers to remember also. And as wives we face a parallel question: How do we look when he comes home at night? Well?

My second suggestion pertains to communication. I guess we could say it in six words: "Listen to him; talk *with* him."

Certainly the children's problems and painting the house and the PTA are important, but you must make the time (you won't just find it) to listen to what your husband wants to talk about. And you must be knowledgeable enough to be able to respond. (More about this knowledge bit later.)

It's vital to be interested in your husband's work, if he wants you to be. Some men want their wives to share this area of life; others do not. But you must make the time for him to do so, if he wants to.

Of course, you might not understand all he is talking about. I don't know much about the oil business except what a tool-joint and a drill collar are, and that is rather limited. But I do need to listen, to let Chuck unload if he wants to. So do we all. We need to be sounding boards; many times people can find answers just by talking about the problem to someone who is unbiased.

Make the time. It may be just after he gets home, it may be just after supper, it may be as soon as the children are in bed. That depends on you and your circumstances. But make the time.

Now about the knowledge bit. You'll need to do some reading. I know a lady with preschool children who can't wait to get them in bed after lunch so she can watch the soap operas. She's having a communication problem with her husband, also, and complains: "Well, I just really don't know enough to talk intelligently on different subjects, so I just don't talk."

For a woman, that's a real tragedy—in many ways.

The reason she doesn't know is because she hasn't read. In the next breath, she told me all the details of each soap opera, and at one point I broke into the conversation (well, monologue, to be honest about it).

"I'm sure that's a great program," I commented. "But you could tune in six months from now, and Mary would still have amnesia— or something like it—and Margaret would still be going to have a baby—or another one. So you can skip the next few months and still not lose the story line."

We need to know what's going on in our world today and to be able to talk about it intelligently. The TV can be a real blessing. If you like it, turn on the early morning show, and you'll get most of the news of the day. Then there are newspapers and magazines.

Scan these at least if you don't have time to read them. You may not be an authority, but at least you'll know that Watergate is not the entrance to a swimming pool.

(And incidentally, the language is changing fast. You don't get spaced out at a Space Center either.)

We've talked about taking a good look at yourself and doing something about it, about making time to listen and to have something to say, and about the importance of keeping up. Then I think my next suggestion would be along more romantic lines—tell him you love and respect him and show it by your actions.

Sounds simple, doesn't it?

It isn't.

You see, we hear it so much—and see it so little—that the words, in part, have lost their meaning.

"Why should I?" you ask, looking around your lovely early American living room. "He hasn't told me he loved me since the days when our furniture was 'early marriage!' "

Maybe he hasn't, but do it anyway. Choose a time and be very loving and kind. It won't hurt the children at all to see you being affectionate toward your husband. A little love pat, or a kiss, gives them a feeling of security that their mom and dad really love each other.

Of course, the man in your life may not notice at first what you're doing. And that's my fifth point. If he doesn't, give him time. The first time you decide to go up and put your arms around him and say, "I love you, honey," he may respond, "What do you want?"

Now listen! He may have his mind on something else, or he may be a little embarrassed because this hasn't happened in a while, or he may respond in some way you had not anticipated at all. That's one of the wonderful things about being married—you never get so adjusted that you can't be surprised. It does make it interesting. Sometimes I almost wish it were less interesting!

I can remember occasions when I have told Chuck something that was very, very important and gave him all the details. He was sitting there, overstuffed, in the overstuffed chair, looking in

my direction. When I finished my bit of exciting news, I'd ask:
"Well, what do you think?"

There would be an abrupt silence, and then his eyes would focus
suddenly. "Uhhh . . . We'll have to see about that, honey." He
hadn't heard a word.

You think to yourself, I'll kill him when he goes to sleep tonight . . . I surely will! But after a few moments, you know this
wouldn't be the solution. Everyone takes such a dim view of it,
and murder's so messy.

Anyway, do be patient with him. He doesn't know you're on
this self-improvement plan, so he doesn't know how to react. Give
him time. He'll come around. They always do.

The last point I want to make cannot be overemphasized. Mrs.
G. did not mention her church, her God, or her spiritual life, and
I wondered about it. From my personal experience, I can tell you
that having the Lord as a partner in your marriage is the most important thing in keeping a home together and keeping it loving.

Chuck and I had a happy marriage for about ten or fifteen years.
We loved each other devotedly. He was trying his best to get
ahead; I was trying just as hard to make the kind of home he wanted.

Then, through the influence of the Billy Graham team who came
to Houston in 1952, a change came into our lives. Because of a
mutual friend, we came to know the team very well—Grady Wilson,
Bev Shea, Cliff Barrows, and Billy Graham himself. Every night
after the Crusade, some of us would take cake and homemade ice
cream down to their hotel, and we'd all visit together. Chuck
and I came to see firsthand what a fabulous thing the Christian life
could be, and we had a yearning—almost a hurting—inside to know
the Lord better. But we didn't tell each other.

Later, when he was in Oklahoma City and I was in Houston, one
Saturday morning in our little house on Quenby Street, I knelt
down and said: "Lord, I want you to come into my life in a real
way. I want the joy I saw in those people's faces and in the way
they act. I want you to come into all my life—into our home, into
our marriage, into every phase of activity that my life touches. I

want you in it all."

In Oklahoma City, on that same morning, Chuck knelt and said: "Lord, take my life and make it count for you. Be real in my marriage, in my career, in my social life, in everything."

That's how it came about. And it was wonderful! We shared with each other later what had happened, and it added a third dimension to our marriage. I can't say exactly how it all evolved. I just know we asked God to do it, and he did.

Our marriage took on a glow; it took on love in a much broader sense. From that time on, the romance has never gone out of our marriage.

These are just six suggestions, but they're not really new. Paul verbalized them a long time ago in the thirteenth chapter of First Corinthians.

Love suffers long, and is kind . . .

Love seeks not her own, is not easily provoked . . .

Bears all things, hopes, endures . . .

Love never fails . . .

That's what real romance is all about.

8
Frilly Formals and Jeans with Jelly—Daughters!

Funny thing about problems. They may come in pairs or even in trios, like the time the sudden shower descended when you were wearing that new fad, a paper dress.

And then, of course, your umbrella sprang a big leak.

Well, maybe *sprang* isn't quite the right word. The leak is there, a big hole in the umbrella that you had forgotten all about. But when the water starts running down your back, you remember the day that your daughter, your scissors, some new material, and the umbrella all got together in what proved to be a rather unfortunate way.

"Oh, Mommy, I am so sorry! I was using your nice little umbrella to sort of anchor down the edge of my material—and I didn't know that I cut right into it also. I'm so sorreeeeee!" And the young voice dissolved in tears.

Before you knew it, you were putting your arms around her telling her it was all right, that you didn't need that old umbrella anyway. (This was the one you bought and hid for six weeks because you were afraid your husband would see it and remember how much it cost.)

But little girls are great, and big ones are, too, or perhaps the better phraseology would be "more mature ones." In the beginning when the girl-type cherubs arrive, there may be some disappointed papas when the nurse announces, "It's a girl!" If so, don't worry. It won't take that little one long to make putty out of papa.

Some papas start out being putty where little girls are concerned.

I remember when our daughter Gay was born. She was our second child, and I had thought it would be something like the time Chuck, Jr., our first, made his decidedly vocal entry into the world. It wasn't. But let me tell you about our firstborn so you'll understand what I mean.

Several times on houseparty programs I have followed a lovely lady who speaks beautifully and eloquently, with ease and with poise. To make matters worse, she looks the part. Her name is Mrs. Woodson Armes. Standing in front of hundreds of girls, she is lovely and small and petite, as well as another word that comes to mind—elegant.

And then there's me. My hairdo is not elegant or even casual— it might better be described as "casualty." I'm sure my fingernail polish is chipped, and I must have a runner in my hose. That's the way I feel when I look at her.

Mrs. Armes, in speaking of the joys of motherhood, would say: "And they laid that lovely little piece of pink and white humanity in my arms. I looked down at this lovely little baby, part of me and part of my husband, and said, 'Oh, what a beautiful baby.' "

Well, my experience was a little different from that of Mrs. Armes. The nurse did come in with my first child, a baby boy, and laid him in my arms. Pink and white? No, he was red, wrinkled, and squalling. And did I say, "What a beautiful baby?" No, I think my comment ran something like "What—this is a baby?"

Remembering Chuck, Jr.'s advent into the world—and, by the way, he has turned out to be a very fine-looking young man—I may have been expecting something of the same thing when our daughter, Gay, arrived. I do recall thinking when they placed her in my arms that she just couldn't be ours because she was so little, so petite, so dainty. I looked down at that indescribably sweet little girl in my arms and then up at my husband who was leaning over us. His blue eyes filled with tears which dripped off on the little blanket and he put his arms around both of us and said: "Marge, God's given us a little daughter. Thank you, Lord, for our little girl. Help us to rear her to love you and to be near you. You've done a wonderful thing for us, God!"

Yes, I look back on that night, and it brings a warm feeling deep inside of me even today.

Someone has said that little girls are the nicest things that happen to people, and they really *are*! They are born with a little angelic glow about them. Though this glow may wear thin at times, there is always enough left to run off on your heart even when their face is covered with peanut butter, or they sob dramatically, or they wear mother's best shoes and dress through the mud!

A little girl can absolutely run you ragged, drive you up the wall, and melt your heart . . . all at the same time! She can giggle for hours and talk incessantly, and you want to climb the curtains. (Don't, unless you've been on Weight Watchers longer than I have.) Yet when you open your mouth to tell her just what the score is (though, of course, you don't know yourself), she stands there so quietly, with a "look of love," that you forget what you were going to say!

Girls come in five colors—black, white, red, yellow, or brown. Mother Nature must be pretty smart—she matches you up perfectly!

A little girl just *loves* birthday parties, little fuzzy kittens, kindergarten, her friends, paper-dolls, play-likin', cooking with Mother, coloring books, lipstick, puzzles, and boys!

She really isn't crazy about company, big animals, big chairs, spinach, lizards, snakes, or staying in the house. She squeals at just *anything,* knows when she's made you nervous, is terribly occupied when it's time to go to bed, and tongue-tied when you want to show her off!

As she grows older, the changes come quickly! Before you know it, she's spending most of her time in jeans and T-shirts, her face is dirty, and she shampoos her hair three times a week!

God seems to have given little girls a beautiful built-in faith in himself. She understands, without questioning, that God is good and merciful, yet so great and powerful! She seems to sense the great potential that he has placed in her! She knows that in his plan of life she plays a *very* important part!

Girls don't seem to mind soap and water, too much, like boys do. They don't seem to mind baths, and they come from baths looking so fresh and lovely! Yet it is important that every girl come to understand how a boy feels about his coating of grime. If she doesn't, she may make the mistake in later years of burning her husband's bathrobe just about the time it was well broken in.

What do girls do? They quickly become young women right before your very eyes! Very early in their lives they begin to stand before the mirror and look at themselves, and evaluate the face and figure as if they were looking at a completely different person (and let me say right here that that song "Wishing Will Make It So" is not exactly accurate). Our young lady will stand before the mirror and smile in various ways. Then she will give her reflection a melting look, a sultry look, the whole bit, and decides which ones she likes the best. After a while, she'll acquire that "perfect way" she wants to look, and we'll realize that "our young lady" is certainly growing up! She also learns the art of manipulation! She'll need it later, so she practices on her Daddy for years! And then the young men can't understand how she *knows* so much about them!

I'm glad we've had a daughter—Chuck and I—and we are very proud of Gay. She has become everything her mother and dad wanted her to be. Her teenage years were quite normal; they had their times of being rough around the edges. In remembering these days, in thinking through it all again, I started wondering what I would do differently if the opportunity were mine again.

Basically, what I would try to do would be to equip her for life in a better fashion. Today we use the expression "Tell it like it is." I think I'd try to help my daughter "See it like it is."

Perhaps a good starting point would be to be honest with myself and her. How much of what I want for her is to gratify my own selfish ambitions, perhaps unfulfilled, and how much for her?

I remember when Gay was about sixteen years old and we were living in West Texas. We had just moved there, and she was having a hard time getting acquainted. After a while when friendships began to develop, the thought occurred to me, Wouldn't it be great if

Gay would be a cheerleader and then she'd get to know everyone and have a fantastic time!

Gay is quieter than I and my thinking was: Oh, she just needs to be brought out. She needs to be doing this, and she needs to be doing that. So I was always trying to push her into doing things.

One day I sprang my idea. "Now, Gay, I've thought of what would be just a great thing for you. Here's what you do. You go out for cheerleader because if you make it, you'll meet everyone in school and have so much fun!"

And I went on and on at considerable length telling her all about it.

She listened, but then she said quietly, "Mother, I just don't want to be a cheerleader."

"It's just because you've never been one, Gay. You'll enjoy it once you get into it. And I'll help you." I was quite firm in my suggestions.

She let me go on a little longer and when I got all through she said, still speaking quietly: "Well, Mother, that's all right for you if you want to be a cheerleader, but you see, I don't want to be another Marge Caldwell. I just want to be Gay. Please let me."

Inside of me a little voice was saying, "Marge, do you want this for Gay, or are you trying to push your own ambitions into her life?"

From that experience I tried to learn a lesson and let her be Gay Caldwell, her own wonderful self.

Then I think I would watch for my daughter's talents, her strong points, and seek to help her develop these. If she had weaknesses, I would want to help her face them squarely. To know oneself is important—to accept oneself is most important of all. I would do all that I could to help her know herself and to find self-acceptance.

I would want to teach her right from wrong. This may sound elementary, but in today's world young people are told so often that "everything is gray—nothing is either black or white." True, the gray area is expansive and expensive indeed, but the blacks and whites are still there.

Tying in with this, I would teach her to honor truth and honesty, to practice honesty herself, and to respect it in others.

I would help her to understand the exciting meaning of freedom. Freedom is not speeding down the highway and getting away with it! It is respecting authority and obeying the law, for this is what makes for freedom from fear. And, interestingly enough, the same laws we strengthen by upholding, also protect us!

I think it would be important for her to know that the girl who will do *anything* to be accepted by her peers is not always the popular girl in the long run. It is the young lady with self-respect who is sought after, ultimately. If she doesn't respect herself, she cannot expect anyone else to! And they won't!

I would want her to meet her responsibilities and be the kind of person who is dependable, remembering that reputation is what others think of you, and character is what you really are!

Of course I would want her to learn to cook and to sew, although I realize I'm not much of an example in these areas. (I did make a dress one time in the seventh grade. As long as I was walking toward you, it was fine. But all the extra material I bunched up together and tied with a sash in the back. That must have been the year I was a very forward girl.)

Seriously, to be able to cook, to sew, and to know how to run a home smoothly, all of these are decided assets.

Finally, and through it all, I would surround my daughter with my love. I would help her to understand on a day-to-day basis by what I said and also by what I did that I loved her for herself, as an individual, as someone well worthy of love. I would seek her confidence and not betray it. Through the years I would value the lines of communication and seek to keep them open.

Above all, I would want to give her the basis of a strong faith in God, remembering that she must have this for a starting point all of her life. I would lead her to accept Jesus Christ as her Savior and help her to find that "life more abundant." I would remember Proverbs 22:6 which says, "Train up a child in the way he should go: and when he is old, he will not depart from it." I'd tuck that verse deep in my heart so that I'd know God will bring her back if she strays from him.

What are little girls made of?

Really, there's no recipe, for God makes each one a little different!

And the wonderful part about his recipes (and how they differ from mine) is that they work if properly followed!

'Nuff said!

9
From the Mouths of Babes

So many times in our lives we have the most terrible things happen to us, and we wish we could disappear in a hole somewhere! Remember your most embarrassing moment? Remember when the hair on the back of your neck would literally stand on end when you or someone in your family would do or say something horrible?

When our firstborn, our son, Chuck, Jr. was born, we were in for years of excitement, embarrassment, joy, confusion, and the most *fun* any family could experience! Mother had often said that it was good that Chuck, Sr. and I married each other, and didn't ruin two households! It's always been a circus at our house—laughter, joy, fusses, hilarity, togetherness, lots of humor—along with the serious moments of love, admiration, respect, and deep, deep devotion!

Children bring blessings into the home along with the problems and concerns! Sometimes these blessings are easily overlooked and lost amid the problems of clothes, school, sicknesses, grades, PTA, homeroom activities, bills, and building a marriage and family! But those blessings are there, and so many times they are stored in our minds for future reference and recall! So now let's you and I get comfortable, relax, and laugh a little as I disclose to you some of the truly funny things said at our house while you recall some of the same you experienced!

Chuck, Jr. (or little Chuck, as we called him, which is the most terrible thing in the world one can do to their offspring) was the type child who told the truth no matter the consequences. He even told the truth when nobody had asked for it! In fact he told everything in the world he had heard at home and elsewhere, and if the interest was running high, his imagination would take over! We aged a million years when he'd start out with, "You know what my mother said about you?" or "My daddy said that you . . ." or "Is she that lady . . . ?" He had many faults, but he always volunteered information which was truthful, we could always depend on *that!*

We were living in Kansas for the first few years of his life, and when he was about four years old, we came home for a visit. We were going for a hamburger for lunch—my mother, her good friend, one of our kinfolks, Chuck, and I. We were riding along enjoying being together. Chuck leaned over to me, and with a loud whisper (his whisper sounded like a small scream) he said: "Mother, does God punish you if you think something but you don't say it?"

"Why, no!" I replied, "What on earth are you thinking, honey?"

It got deathly quiet in the car, and he pointed to our member of the family and said, "I was just thinking how dumb Mrs. . . . looked!"

Of course you can imagine what followed. I ate him up one side and down the other, but the damage was done! He is in his mid-thirties now, and just the other day that lady remarked, "I wonder if I still look as dumb to Chuck as I did when he was four?"

One day he was playing at the other end of the block with a little friend his age. All of a sudden I heard him screaming and running home: "Mother! Mother! Get out the belt! Get out the belt!"

I ran out to see what was the matter, and he cried: "Get the belt! I just spit all over William. I spit in his hair, on his clothes, and as soon as I get some more spit, I'm going to spit all over his face!"

I got out the belt. But if Chuck had known what was in my heart, he'd have known my heart wasn't in that whipping! I was about to die laughing inside!

One day I took him to the doctor for a checkup when we were living in Oklahoma City. He was about eight years old. I don't guess he was ever still, even when he was asleep. We nearly went crazy with his eternal wiggling and squirming. He talked incessantly and asked millions of questions. I was complaining to the doctor about how I couldn't keep him still and quiet. (One day after Christmas Chuck took our old discarded Christmas tree and planted it in our new yard. I had left him with a sitter and she was busy, so he gathered Christmas trees from all the neighborhood and planted them in our yard. Can you imagine what our yard looked like when I returned? Another time he shut our Persian cat up in the washing machine to protect her from our dog. He neglected to tell anyone what he'd done. Later that day I went to the washing machine to do some laundry, opened the lid, and out sprang a large mass of fur! As it whizzed past me, I almost fainted. These weren't spasmodic incidents, they were continual!)

As I shared this with our doctor, he laughed and said: "Mrs. Caldwell, you'd better watch this kid! He could go either way!"

One day when he was ten, he came home from school for lunch. Gay, our youngest, and Chuck and I were eating lunch and he looked up at me and said: "Mother, tell me about sex."

I swallowed hard, and said, "What do you want to know, honey?"

"*All* about it," he replied.

So I assured him that his Daddy wanted to answer all his questions himself, so that evening when Daddy returned, he could talk to him. That seemed to satisfy him, and I laughed inside when I thought of Chuck, Sr. with his first lesson in sex coming up. That evening at dinner Chuck, Jr. said,

"Daddy, I want you to tell me all about sex."

Chuck, Sr. was just about to drink his coffee, and he almost swallowed his cup!

"What part do you want to know, son?" in his most intellectual tone of voice.

"Just start at the beginning and don't leave out anything!"

So Chuck Jr. and Sr. went out on the front porch to talk and I began clearing the table! Oh, how I wanted to listen! In less than ten minutes, Chuck, Sr. walked in, and I laughed and asked: "Is that all the time it took for you to tell him all about sex?"

Chuck looked very nonplussed and laughed: "Marge, I was trying so hard to tell it right and make him understand, and right in the middle of a sentence, he yelled: "Golly, Daddy, there's Jimmy! I'm gonna play some catch."

Each day brought a new experience. One morning when he was quite young, about nine years old, he was outside playing. He came into the house, looking solemn, and asked: "Mother, if you die, will my daddy marry again?"

My heart nearly broke. Why, there was my precious little boy, playing out there in the sandpile, and worrying about my dying. I assured him that I was going to live quite a long time, that I was *very* healthy.

In a few minutes he returned. "Mother, but if you *do* die, will my daddy marry again?"

I stooped down, gathered him in my arms and in my most soothing voice assured him again that I would be around a long time.

"Why are you worrying about my dying?" I asked.

"Well, I just wondered," he said, "cause if you do, I sure hope Daddy marries someone like Betty Grable next time!"

Now if you don't happen to be old enough to know who Betty Grable is, she was the glamour girl of that day, and that didn't do much for my ego!

Then after so many years the college days came! Our son attended Rice University. During his sophomore year we were living in Midland, Texas. One night we got a call from Chuck: "Dad, I'm in the emergency room at Methodist Hospital!"

We nearly died with fright. When Chuck could speak, he asked what had happened.

"Well, you see, a bunch of us boys were at the library studying. One of them bet me that I couldn't jump off the balcony of the library, and they took up ten dollars between them to see if I could! Well, Dad, you know how it is! I *had* to try, and besides, I needed that money. So I jumped, and somehow my knees collided with my nose, and it's broken. My nose, that is!"

Of course, it cost us about a hundred dollars, but he won ten dollars! We never could figure that one out! Maybe we're just on a different wave length!

I know I don't have heart trouble! If I did, I'd have died long ago from fright! One night while Chuck, Jr. was in college and living at home, I had a friend over for coffee. Chuck, Sr. was working, and Gay wasn't home. Chuck, Jr. was studying upstairs in his room. At least that was where I thought he was! You could come downstairs and walk into the den and go outside without being seen from the living room. And that's exactly what he did. We were sitting in the living room as calm as could be, and all of a sudden my friend became ashen and seemed almost paralyzed with fright! I asked her what was the matter, and she simply couldn't speak! I glanced behind me, and Chuck, Jr. had put a stocking over his head, put on his Dad's overcoat and hat, and was walking like Frankenstein toward us! I've often wondered what I'd do when I was so frightened! Well, I can tell you what I'd do! I'd just stand there and scream until my breath was gone! Chuck, Jr. jerked off all of the paraphenalia he had on, and kept saying, "Golly, Mother! Can't you take a joke?"

My friend wasn't the same for days, and for a long time would not come to see me if Chuck, Jr. was home!

But you know! The days and weeks and years passed, and I wouldn't change any of them. We had our times of insurmountable joy and happiness, then we had anxious nights of illness and pain! I guess we always wished we had just a little bit more money, or fewer bills, or another car, or something else. But we began to realize that "things" aren't that important! It's the people in the family that are the important thing! The picnics, the slumber parties that almost undid the whole family, the car-pooling that made me feel no less than a chauffeur most of the school days, the endless telephone conversations, the arguments over the phone, the grounding, the weekly allowances that just were never enough, the dating rules, the discipline (that hurt *us* more than it did *them*) all fit into a picture of a happy family!

The most beautiful things that happened in our family, however, were the priceless times we had our family devotionals. Those were the experiences that formed our love for Jesus and the desire to find his will. Those are the times that Chuck, Sr. and I treasure more than anything in this world. We do not have great riches to pass on to our children, but we have memories of quiet prayer and sharing about what Jesus had done that day for each of us! Jesus became real in a new sense to all of us, and spiritual glue that can never be torn apart put us together in Christ. I remember when Chuck, Jr. was at college, I would rise early and sit in the den and study and pray. One morning while he was living at home, I heard him coming down the stairs. I thought maybe he was sick or something! When I asked what he wanted, he said: "Mother, could I come down here each morning and pray and study with you?"

Can you imagine my joy? We had some moments that I shall always treasure with the Lord. These were the "togetherness" times that I thank God for.

Our daughter, Gay, finally decided to come down early, too, and then Chuck, Sr. too. We laughed and laughed at how we worked into an early devotional time! If Chuck, Sr. had announced that we were going to start such a thing, the kids would have screamed their heads off!

Life is a beautiful experience! How could we possibly appreciate the mountaintop experiences, if we had no valleys to compare them with? I praise God for the family! It is under fire from society in our day, but this is not the first time! And somehow I believe that the institution that God formed himself will be strong enough to stand against man's puny efforts to destroy it. Don't you?

10
Teenage Is Not a Disease

For many years during the early part of our marriage, Chuck and I thought that teenagers had a disease that they had to pass through before they became adults! This feeling developed because we had never had the privilege of being around many teenagers for very long at a time! As God opened doors of service to us in 1952, we became excited about what he would have us do. What did he do? He pushed us right smack-dab in the middle of teenagers! Now, that'll do something for you, especially when your own children were still in elementary school and your concerns ran to peanut butter and jelly sandwiches (ugh!), measles, PTA, recipes, and filling the stomachs of little kids! Not to speak of Brownies, and Little League baseball, and Scouts! The transition from those things to pimply skin, dating, broken hearts, parent problems, emotional upheavals (or I should say emotional earthquakes), and moral decisions, really sent us reeling!

Chuck and I had to learn quickly and the hard way that there was no such thing as "puppy love" which we had in the past spoken so glibly about. We had to learn that this was as serious to our young friends as some of the most pressing problems *we* had! We had to learn, too, when we entered the teenage world, that we were entering another culture. The culture shock we suffered was similar to the one people suffered when moving overseas! Another phrase that we had to remove completely from our vocabulary was "When I was a girl—or boy" because nothing is even similar to "when I was a girl!" in these changing times.

That was in 1952. And God has allowed us to stay in the world of these precious young people, much to our own amazement! How the times are changing still, but with much more rapidity. It almost makes your head reel off your shoulders when you think of it. We hardly recognize the changes in looking back—they happened so fast. But they're there, and just shaking our head, tsk-ing in our cheeks, and looking discouraged or disgusted will not make it go away, and bring back the good old days.

Who in the world in their right mind would want back the good old days, anyway? They never *were* as good as we remember them really. I don't know about you, but I'm enjoying all the lovely modern conveniences, the great modes of travel, the excitement of actually living in these changing times. Of course, we all know how much suffering, disease, poverty, and heartache that so many are having today—but it's always been so—even Jesus commented on that. On the other hand, the challenge to serve a living Savior effectively, to relieve suffering where we find it, the answers to disease that are coming so rapidly, the wonder to share not only our means, but the wonderful news of the gospel—oh, just the wonder of living in the "now" is as thrilling and exciting as never before in history!

That makes me think again, seriously, about our young people of today. When you find a moral, intelligent young person of today with real integrity, you should thank God with all your heart for him or her. You see, it's not the easiest thing in the world today to be that kind of person, even for the strongest of them. One day I remarked to a group of adults in their fifties that I thought the young person of today is stronger than we were when we were that same age. One of the men in the group differed with me.

"When I was this age, we had drinking, and necking, and all the temptations that they have now," he said.

I reminded him that in those past years we had the strength of society on our side. Society did not accept the unmarried pregnant girl, premarital sex, drug addiction, drunkenness, filthy movies (no matter how "real" they were), and four letter words used in public.

Now it's all different. The virgin will often hide the fact because she doesn't want to be made fun of; the intellect with good grades just cringes for fear his peers will find out and make snide remarks; and four letter words are a dime a dozen inside *and* outside of the movies.

Many years have passed since 1952, and many experiences have been suffered and enjoyed since then. Chuck and I have been disillusioned in some young people, that's true, but the fantastic numbers that have thrilled our hearts and brought indescribable excitement to our lives so far outweigh the others that it's hardly worth mentioning the ones that have disillusioned us.

There was also a serendipity to all of this! As we learned to cope, or try to cope, with so many of their problems and dilemmas, we found that we came to understand our own children so much better. When our kids became teenagers, we were almost prepared for some of the things we'd encounter. And every little thing helped, because we had learned through our young friends that "teenage is *not* a disease" but a very real, and oftimes very trying time in the growth and development of a person.

As I look back, however, it was the opportunity of introducing Christ to some of them and of helping them to grow and mature in him that blessed our lives immeasurably! As we tried to make Jesus real to them, we found a new level of love and abundant life that we'd never dreamed of! How does one thank a host of teenagers and college students whom God has let touch our lives for the beauty and joy that they have brought to us? How in the world do you say thank you to so many young peop e who showed us with their simple faith that miracles still do happen in this old, battered, torn-apart world of ours? What is more beautiful to behold than the light of Christ in the eyes of a high school senior who the year before had been torn with spiritual confusion, or the optimism and faith of a teenager who lost her leg to cancer, or the college student who rises to unbelievable heights in a time of crisis?

Many problems arise in families that are experiencing the teenage years, in fact, hardly a family escapes. I think the most prevalent one centers around communication, or the lack of it! I get many letters from teenagers asking how I would suggest their "getting through to their parents," others asking "why parents are so unreasonable," and others thinking about leaving home. Many others are raked with grief because of the drinking problem with one or both of their parents, and still others are from teenagers worried sick because of the unfaithfulness of one or other of their parents . . . . and on and on! But this is certainly not a one-sided issue. I get many letters, too, from parents of young people— heartbroken, embarrassed, humiliated, incredulous!

Phrases like: "How on earth could they do this to us?" "What have we done to deserve this?" "How can we get through to our son?" "Where did we make our mistake?" "It's breaking our hearts to see what's happening!" And on and on! Oh, the heartbreak of noncommunication! But this doesn't start when our children are fifteen years old! We can't just turn a knob and the communication starts. It starts in the first years of our children's lives, and it must be worked at and developed daily! To be a parent is not the easiest thing in the world, and it deserves our best efforts! In the world in which we live, there are hundreds of things vying for our children's attention, but God gives us several years with them in the home to form a firm base. They *have* to have this base or there is no place to return to when indecision and temptation comes along!

How many times have I talked to a teenager who said: "My mother (or my grandmother) used to say, 'I'm praying for you while you are gone,' and it would make me so mad. But I never could forget it or forget the look on Mother's face!"

Because I love the teenager so much, and believe in him with all my heart, and because I believe that most parents really love their teenager although they may not understand a lot of what they see and hear, I want to share some ideas about how to keep the lines of communication open between the two of you. These are not great, theological truths but are simple rules of good sense, many of which came straight out of the book of Proverbs in the Old Testament. Funny thing! God has the answers to every one of our dilemmas, if we'd just take the time to find out what he has said about it! So let's take a look and see what we can find out.

First, I'd like to mention a few ways to lose communication with your teenager, mentioning ways teenagers can ruin the communication with parents also. Okay? Ready? Here goes!

1. *Use of sarcasm by parents*
    - *"Anybody* ought to know better than *that!"*
    - "You're acting just like you're two years old! Where's your baby bottle?"
    - It's devastating to a teenager to be "put down" (talked sarcastically to) in front of his peers.
    - The smart parent will wait until alone with his teenager to discipline him or her if it is at all possible!
    - The use of sarcasm is a cowardly way to reprimand your child and causes them to lose respect for you and for your discipline.

    Use of sarcasm by teenagers
    - Never use sarcasm to belittle your parents: for example, "my old lady" or "my old man."
    - Do not act in front of your friends as if your parents are stupid, using gestures, words, looks of disgust—*you* know what I mean!
    - Do not betray your parents by discussing them at school with your friends, laughing at their weaknesses and failures.

2. *Public embarrassment of teenager by parent*
    - If you know that show of affection in public is embarrassing to them, refrain from it.
    - Do not try to monopolize conversation with their date or act in an immature way when they have company.
    - Be sure that you are friendly, yet not trying to be "cute" and entertain their friends. This really embarrasses young people!

    Public embarrassment of parent by teenager
    - Do not contradict your parents in front of their friends.

This will embarrass them beyond measure. Talk to them
about it later. Mother used to say to me, "If you hear me
say the moon is green, you keep quiet, and we'll talk about
it later!"

—Do not talk impudently to your parents, especially in front
of their friends. This not only disgusts the friend about
your parents, but shocks them that you got away with it!
People begin to lose respect for you, too!

—Do not ignore the fact that you have been spoken to. Be
courteous and reply, even if you're about to bite yourself
because someone has said, "My, how you've grown!"
(What did they expect? you're thinking!)

3. *Register of shock by parent*

—Under no conditions register shock by raised eyebrows,
quickly drawn in breath, grimacing (various facial expressions that betray). We can help the expressions that flit
across our faces at times, but we certainly cannot control
the fact that when we're frightened or shocked, the pupils
of our eyes dilate! Now, I teach my classes that poise is
the ability to control oneself in a crisis or an unexpected
situation. We can control all else, but not the pupils of
our eyes! So when I'm flying and the plane begins to make
a funny noise or doing something that seems abnormal to
me, I simply call the stewardess over. I make her get very
close so I can see the pupils of her eyes, and then I know
whether to get concerned or not!

—Never use a previous moment of confidence by your teenager to press home a point. This makes them sorry they
ever confided in you at all! It will probably close the door
to any future confidences.

—Never register shock especially in the first discussions of
sex. Your hair may want to stand on end at some of the
things your child will say, but just spray it heavily, hold on
to your chair, and plunge in! When your child becomes a
teenager, *most* anything might be said. Be ready for the

incredulous look you will get when your teenager realizes
that you and your mate have done "that" or the horrible
embarrassment you feel when they didn't knock and
caught you!

Register of shock by teenager

—You must realize that it's not the easiest thing in the world
  to be a parent. When your parent seems ill at ease in the
  discussion of sex, don't make it hard on them by acting
  shocked at what they say or how they say it. Remember,
  they didn't talk freely about sex like you do, and it's hard
  for them to shift gears in this area.

—When you see your parent acting or talking in a way that
  shocks you, at the right time, sit down and ask them why
  they did this. If you can tell them how it affected you, a new
  understanding may follow, and you can talk more freely
  about some of your other hangups, and theirs as well.

4. *On being a dogmatic parent*

   —The more sure we are about our stand on a subject, the less
     dogmatic we have to be. If you feel that you are being
     reasonable, then you can more easily listen to the opinions
     of others, particularly your teenager.

   —There is a lot of difference between the courage of our con-
     victions and just plain stubbornness. Let's be sure which
     one it is . . . not colored with pride!

   —Conviction brings compassion, and compassion brings
     communication—this is good to remember.

   —When we're wrong, we should admit our mistakes, not
     rationalize. They already see through it, and to say "I'm
     sorry" is one of the greatest tests of maturity! We grow
     ten feet tall in the eyes of our teenager. They already
     know that there's not a person on earth who can be right
     all the time!

On being a dogmatic teenager

—Be sure when we want something, that we're not stubborn
  with our reasoning.

—Do not rationalize your mistakes. Your parents will be
  much more lenient than you think if you will admit that
  you're wrong!
—Remember that the surer you are about what you believe,
  the sweeter you can be when someone differs with you.
  It's when you're not sure that you tend to come unglued
  when you're challenged.

5. *On bluffing as a parent*
  —One of the most disgusting things a parent can do is bluff
    their teenager. As I said before, they know when you do
    this, they can spot it a country mile! We tend to lose re-
    spect for the opinions of those who bluff their way around!
  On bluffing as a teenager
  —You must remember that each parent alive has already been
    along the road you're traveling. They've already used all
    those same excuses, rationalized just like you do, told
    "those little white lies" and half truths. Do you ever
    wonder how in the world they caught on? Well, teenager,
    they've been there before and know all the road signs!
  —Bluffing probably does more to make a parent tend not
    to trust their teenager than anything else. Wouldn't it make
    the same thing happen to you, too?

6. *Negative approach as a parent*
  —Youth is so wonderful because they have not learned to
    say "It won't work" or "We've never done it this way be-
    fore." One of their most thrilling attributes is that they
    are positive and enthusiastic and full of optimism. They
    will automatically reject negativism.
  —You just about get from your teenager what you expect.
    Challenge them as little children to be the best person
    they possibly can be. That's all God asks of them. And
    yet as parents, we sometimes want to make them be a
    reflection of ourselves or the person we'd hoped to be!
    They weren't born to be an extension of ourselves, but a
    dynamic expression of their own personhood. Challenge

them to be *their* best!

Negative approach as a teenager

—Don't make up your mind that you're not going to like the
thing that your parent will suggest! Or that just because
your parents like a certain friend, an idea, or a situation
it will be the worst possible thing that could happen to you!
When you're in your early twenties, you're going to be surprised at how smart your parents have become!

—Remember that your parents are people, and that they're
probably doing the best that they know how to do! Now,
they may make some glaring mistakes, but they do love
you and want you not to make the same mistakes they did!

7. *Can you take a difference of opinion as a parent?*

—How are the rules of discipline and dating, etc., decided in
your home? Are they just handed arbitrarily down to your
teenager because you're the parent and don't "want any
talkback?" Remember that if you make the rules together
and decide on the discipline together, most of the time the
teenager will be harder on himself than you would have
been on him. They are mighty fair when they have a part
in the rule-making. Each side will have to give a little. Remember that if you give in on some of the more insignifi-
cant things, that when the big issues are at stake, your teenager will be more amenable to compromise.

Can you take a difference of opinion as a teenager?

—How do you act when your parents differ with you as to
whether you should do something or not? Do you throw a
fit and froth at the mouth? Don't you know a compromise
can be reached much better if you remain calm and try to
talk it over? It'll be hard to control yourself, but it surely
pays off in the long run!

—Do you greet your parents with the phrase *"Everybody's*
doing it." and can't understand their fury and their retort,
"I don't *care* what everybody's doing. I'm just responsible
for *you!"* Well, you see, because everybody's doing it

really isn't a very valid reason for you to do it, now is it? Don't you know some things that everybody's doing that you *know* isn't good or right to do?

I never will forget one evening when Chuck and I were sitting up in bed reading. Gay, our daughter who was fifteen at the time, came running into the bedroom with her best friend Susan: "Mother," she asked, "Can I go with the gang to (a town nearby) to the movie?" Now, Gay knew that town was off limits for her because it had been the scene of some gang fights and some pretty bad scenes. We'd settled that long ago. But I noticed that she brought Susan in with her to ask to do something that she could not do, hoping I'd give in in front of company. When I told her she couldn't do it, but to settle for a movie in our town, she left. But she looked a thousand retorts, and flipped her hair, and did as much as she felt she could get by with without grounding! Later that night when she returned, she came in our room and crawled up in our bed. "You know what Susan said tonight?" Gay asked. "Susan said that you all loved me better than her parents loved her!" "Why, Gay, Susan's parents love her! What do you mean?" I asked. "Well," she replied, "Susan's parents said she could go over there, and they knew it should be off limits! So I want to thank you for not letting me go!" Chuck and I hugged her, sent her off to bed, looked at each other, and thanked God for courage to stick to our guns!

8. *Are you in a hurry as a parent?*

    —It takes time to raise kids! Isn't that a marvelous statement? Well, it's not original, but it's really true, isn't it? When your teenager comes in at midnight and you're sound asleep—or at least pretending to be—it really is rough to hear her say, "Mother, wake up and come in my room, I have something to tell you!" But go—by all means! Most wonderful confidences are given after midnight when experiences are fresh on their minds and eyes are sparkling or tears are apt to flow freely. It's at times like these that you get to know the wonderful person who is your son or daughter! To be in a hurry would be cruel, just because it is 3 AM!

—Don't look at your watch as if you can spare only a few moments more when your teenager is telling you something very important. If you have to pick up your husband in a few minutes, then ask her to ride with you or make a date to talk further at a certain time.

—To me, as a counselor or parent, it is a sinful thing to betray my son or daughter's confidence. This will close more doors than you possibly imagine! I heard a mother at a coffee one morning say to a whole group of ladies: "Do you know what Mary told me last night about that group of girls at school?" Well, she related a story that I'm sure her daughter would *die* if she knew she'd told. And you can be sure her daughter will find out—and that door will be closed forever for that mother!

9. *Parent, listen to their music!*

—*Really* listen! We let most of it go in one ear and out the other! And we're hoping that it will skip going in our ears and driving us crazy! Oh, the loudness of it!

There are many signals as to what is going on in the young person's mind as we listen to their music! The loneliness, the frustration, the fear of so many things, they're all there! One day our teenage Gay walked in, and a friend of ours was criticizing the music of young people, screaming about how meaningless it was and loud above anything you could imagine! Gay listened and then left. Later she came in and asked: "Mother, what were some of the popular songs when you were my age?" I thought for a minute: "Oh, let's see! 'The Music Goes Round and Round and Comes Out Here' and 'Flat Foot Floogie with a . . .'" and then I caught the look on her

face! "Mother, I can't believe you all thought that was
good music!" she laughed as she rolled on the floor! I
compared those songs with "Bridge Over Troubled Waters,"
"Everything Is Beautiful," and "Raindrops," and I saw
what she meant.

—Now some of the modern music is rather bad, if you can
hear the words. Sometimes it's better if we don't, our
hair would come out at the roots! And the beat is deafen-
ing and different! But you and I must remember that they
have never been exposed to some of the lovely music we
grew up with, and you do not appreciate something with
which you are not familiar. Instead of complaining about
their music, see that some beautiful and uplifting music is
played within their hearing. They will finally respond if
they are not "preached at" about their listening habits.
Why do you suppose that some of the most popular songs
at the moment are the caliber of "Amazing Grace" and
oldies like "Night and Day" and "Stardust?" And they
think they are new! There's nothing that finally we won't
come back to one way or another!

Teenager, listen to parent's music!

—Do you really want to know what your parents like? Just
listen to their music! "Oh, it's so corny!" you exclaim,
"I can't *stand* that country western!"

   Listen to it, anyway! No telling what you may find out
about your parents! Do they like the real dreamy, romantic,
type of music? Well, do you see why? Because they're that
type of person! You don't believe it? Just watch and see!
Do they like symphony? And it bores you? Well, it's because they've been taught the meaning behind all the music
and they appreciate it. I'll bet they're pretty knowledgeable
about many cultural things, and you'll appreciate that later.

—We both need to realize that we are products of our rearing!
We were raised with one kind of music, and you were
raised in another atmosphere. There's good and bad in

both environments, so we need to communicate and take the good out of each! Now that's real communicating!

One of the most important things for all of us to remember is that communication works both ways! There is no communication when conversation is one-sided! Just like there is no communication with God when the conversation is one-sided. So many times we talk to him and ask him to bless, help, heal, change, and never sit still and let him talk to us! *Real* communication is exchange of ideas and thoughts, dreams and goals, blessings and sorrows—the whole meaning of life! How sweet it is when we learn how to listen! I do a lot of counseling and have done this for many years. There is such a desperate need for people to listen. The best counseling is listening with an emphatic ear! I remember one afternoon out in West Texas where we were living at that time, the phone rang. When I answered it, a young friend of mine was crying hysterically. Could she please come over and talk to me just a minute? Of course she could! So in a few minutes she came running into the house, sat down on the sofa by me and began to sob! She cried and poured out her story. All I did was sit there quietly and say, "Oh, I'm sorry!" and "Well, a . . .!" and "Oh, dear!" I never really got anything out! In a few minutes she grabbed me around the neck and said: "Oh, thank you, Mrs. Caldwell! You just don't know how much you have helped me!" and she ran out!

Chuck was coming in the back door as she ran out the front. He asked who it was, and I told him. Then I said: "You know, that's the funniest thing! She had a problem and came to tell me about it. I never said a word, and then she grabbed me around the neck and thanked me for helping her!" "Well, Marge," he teased, "I wish you'd counsel with *me* like that." I imagine that's the best counseling I've ever done!

As I'm talking out of my heart to you, I'd have to say that love is the answer to it all! You really have to care! When I think how God so loved that he gave, then I realize that love is really something you do! You can't really love without doing, just like you can't love without being! What a privilege we as parents have to help mold the lives of our children and prepare them for adulthood! And of course we always hope that we've improved on the past. So if I had one wish for each of you, I would wish that communication lines could be kept open between you and your teenager!

Chuck and I couldn't have made it without this promise from God that we kept tucked in our hearts during those years of "growing up." It's Proverbs 3:5-6: "Trust in the Lord with all thine heart; and lean not unto your own understanding. In all thy ways acknowledge him and he shall direct thy paths."

11
You Take the Good Ol' Days—I Don't Want Them

"I'll take the good old days," I heard a man exclaim the other day. "When things made sense!"

I looked up in surprise to see who had made the comment. He wasn't anyone I knew, but there was a certain rigidity about his expression that made me think: You don't have to take the good old days, bud. If that's the way you think, you've already been taken.

The "good old days" is an expression that means different things to different people. Being human (most of us), I suppose we are inclined to look back and remember the good things, to forget the things less pleasant. Sometimes our yesterdays come through the filter of the years with almost a halo effect. (Some of us do need all the halos we can get, but we won't argue that point just now.)

I would not rob anyone of his golden memories, and I have a few myself. But from another viewpoint, when we stop and take a look at yesterday and then at today, some rather startling conclusions seem to emerge.

The remark reminded me of a poem that came out in the *Ladies Home Journal* in 1968. It reflected the change in our language, referring to such words as "hippie," "trip," "pot," "grass," "hooked," and "fix."

Yes, the language is changing, but then so are a number of things. And in many instances, it's a change for good.

I can remember back to many of those "good old days." They were different in some respects. But even then the adults talked about how the children were "going to the dogs." (I wonder how the dogs feel about that?)

And then somewhere just recently I came across a letter written by a worried father about his teenage son who was seemingly headed downhill. It sounded like it might have been written since 1970, but the date on it indicated it was written in the late 1700's. And then I've seen another piece of writing of similar nature: "I just don't know about young people today; I don't know where they're headed, but their behavior concerns me." This little jewel was dated in the 1800's.

So we see that for generations back, the adults have worried about the young people. When I stood on the bridge between the teenage years and young adulthood, I could see something of both sides. It began to dawn on me then (remember that I am a night person and dawn does not come easily) that this pattern just seemed to be the natural concern of the older generation for the young. Maybe the difficulty is that the older ones are so established on what they consider the solid foundations of their days that they're not able to bend a little and see how things really are today.

Certainly there were some good things about the good old days, but let's take another look and see how some of it really was.

I remember back in my courting days (no, this was not King Arthur's court). Just after Chuck and I had decided to get married, my mother, my brother, and I went with my husband-to-be to meet his family.

I had always lived in Houston. (Now that I look back on it, I don't believe that I was ever off the pavement.) But there we were, out on the highway going to Amarillo. Chuck had told me he lived in Bovina.

Well, actually what he first told me was that he lived in Amarillo. But when we got close to Amarillo, he said: "Well, I don't really live in Amarillo. I just said Amarillo because you wouldn't know where this town is, but I really live in Bovina."

When we got to the outskirts of Bovina, a very wondeful little town, Mother said, "Well, Chuck, where do you live?"

Chuck hesitated a moment and then said: "Well, I really don't live in Bovina. I live in a community called Oklahoma Lane."

So we drove through Bovina and out about seven or eight miles to a small community with a school and a couple of churches and a store, the Oklahoma Lane community.

Mother said, "Well, Chuck, where do you live?'

And Chuck said: "I don't really live in the community. We live on a farm outside of Oklahoma Lane."

And so it was that we finally got out to the farm. Seeing it first-hand was something I shall never forget. My mother had been more or less reared on a farm, so she knew what to expect. My brother and I didn't. It was all so completely different.

I never will forget that great big pot-bellied black stove right in the middle of the living room, and everyone gathered around it. Someone had really left the gate open, as they say in the Panhandle, and it was bitterly cold. The stove fascinated me. It was amazing how you could be so hot in the front when you faced it, and so cold on your backside. So you would turn around and back up to it, and then repeat the process all over in reverse. I felt something like a Baked Alaska—one of those fancy desserts that's frozen on the bottom and flaming on top.

Later in the evening we crawled into bed, and oh those cold sheets! They were straight out of the igloo and not even thawed yet. We had four or five blankets or quilts stacked on top of us to keep us warm. I remember that you'd snuggle on down and get a warm place all fixed in the bed but then you couldn't move your foot a half an inch. If you did, you'd freeze to death. So there you'd stay where the warm spot was all night long . . . long . . . long.

That particular trip, as well as many others, has around it the golden glow of a happy memory. But nonetheless, when I sit down in my centrally-heated living room or air-conditioned den, I am grateful again for the modern conveniences that are part of our times.

Then when you crawl into bed under a nice electric blanket and flip on the switch, it's so very, very comfortable. If you're warm-natured and your husband is cold-natured, there are blankets with dual control, and everyone can do his own thing. With gratitude I flip on the switch, remembering at times those five blankets and those icy sheets of days gone by.

Had you ever stopped to think about what a wonderful place a bathroom is? To be able to take a nice warm bath in a comfortable room, to be able to brush your teeth and fix your face and put on your makeup or shave—whatever you do—in either heat or air conditioning, whatever you need. That's a miracle in itself. There were times, they tell me, when the bathroom was one or two hundred feet outside the back door. It may have been hot and humid, cold and windy, or pouring down rain, yet the bathroom didn't come any closer.

Surely things are different today, and much of it is an improvement. A part of our problem is that perhaps we have not kept up with the pace and the language.

I am thinking just now of a friend of mine in Midland who is a grandmother. She tells me that she needs to get her twelve-year-old grandson to read the funnies for her, not because she has a literacy problem but because now she can't be sure of understanding what she reads.

The thought comes to me that this may be one of the major difficulties. We need to keep up, so we can enjoy our lives day by day. The pace is hectic, but I believe I would rather wear out than rust out.

Sometimes when we just sit back and criticize and gripe, we need to step out of ourselves (a good idea in many ways) and take a good look. Have we kept up? Do we need to change our method of doing things;

Memories are great, but they are the by-products of happy times, not the daily bill of fare. Unless we create some great memories today by living today, tomorrow will be awfully short-changed in the memory department. Surely, with inflation spiralling, we don't need change any shorter than it is!

Perhaps we resist change because of two reasons: We don't

understand the new way of doing things, and we are comfortable in the little rut—our daily habit. But if we don't scramble out of the rut, how can we ever see what is just over the rim of the hill?

How do you really feel about life? The present time can be the greatest time of all, regardless of our age, if we will just let it be.

This seems to be a very natural thing with many young people. In fact there is a musical entitled *Natural High* which tells of the tremendous exhilaration a young person can experience who lets the Lord live in him and through him. Teenagers feel for the most part that life is exciting. Since there is so much to be done, so much to be experienced, so many wonderful times to have, let's be sure we spend wisely the coin called today.

Now if you are a teenager, you're probably thinking: Well, life is just pretty exciting. I've got it all before me and I don't want to waste a bit of it.

You're right. You do have it all before you, and you don't want to waste any. And because you don't, take care of yourself. Don't throw away your wealth. Take care of your mind—don't blow it. Feed it well, and it will do the same for you in some tomorrow.

Take care of your body. Don't blow it on drugs, liquor, or sex, as though you had no respect for yourself. The Bible tells us that our bodies are the temple of the Holy Spirit. What kind of a temple have you invited him into?

Don't blow your mind, don't blow your body, and love your neighbor as yourself.

As who?

That's right—as yourself. You are important. Don't sell yourself short. You cannot love someone else properly unless you can respect yourself, and that gets us back to where we started.

Adults, how do you really feel about life?

"Oh, my soul," you say, "here I am rushing to get breakfast ready, to get the kids off to school on time and my husband off to work, to get down to the church for a group meeting, and then to the community nursery for the board meeting, to get to a luncheon for the next United Fund drive, and then to the grocery store because it's double stamp day and I need to get there before the kids get out of school—all of this, and you want to know how I feel about life? I feel snowed—that's how I feel!"

In this sense perhaps the "good old days" did have an advantage. But even with all the pressures of today's living, we needn't be jumping up and down like a yo-yo with the seven year itch.

A church bulletin I once saw put it this way: "There are three things Jesus never did—he never worried; he never hurried; he never doubted the outcome."

This thought, a basic one, is true regardless of the age in which we live. Each day brings its own unique sorrows and joys. But if we have a vital relationship with the Lord, we know that through all the tragedy and heartache, God is ever our help and our peace. In times of joy, he shares our happiness.

Notice this is for the present and for the future.

"Now is the accepted time," the Bible says. "Now is the day of salvation" (2 Cor. 6:2).

Now is the day to begin the abundant life that Jesus has told us we can have. For just as we can rust out our minds sighing for the good old days, we can rust out our spirits by simply sitting still and not acting upon God's promises.

The good old days were great but today is greater. I believe I'd rather have a ten-speed bike than a bicycle built for two to travel in today's world.

12
Cold Facts About
a Hot Problem — Drugs

"Mrs. Caldwell, what's wrong with smoking a little pot? Why do people get so uptight about it?"

"Tell me, Marge, what really happens with heroin?"

Drugs are making the scene today in a way that's unreal, but it's unreeling, nonetheless. It's happening mostly to the "now generation" but quite a few others are involved as well.

Maybe this is one of those cases in which we wish history would repeat itself, because in 1914, when the Harrison Act was passed, only one person in 400 was a narcotics addict. Today, some authorities say there are over 500,000 heroin addicts—which equates it with the worst period in American history.

But there's something different today that is vastly disturbing. Today's addict is not the typical adult, white, southern male—many of whom became addicted through medication in other years—but the typical addict today is a ghetto minority group teenager. . . plus those in every category you can imagine!

Research done in this area also shows us that there is a decided connection between drugs and crime. Among lawbreakers who used drugs, the breakdown in one study went something like this: Marijuana was the highest—28 percent of the people who committed major crimes and were drug users were using "Mary Jane" at the time; heroin—24 percent; barbituates—17 percent; cocaine—10 percent; amphitamenes—9 percent; hashish—9 percent; psycadelica—5 percent; and so on down to tranquilizers, glue, etc.

Why?

We used to say, "That's the sixty-four dollar question." But with inflation there's no telling what the question would be worth today. That's not important. What does matter is the answer. A part of it we know; the rest we don't.

Why? What makes for the hold that drugs have on some of our teenagers today?

At the risk of oversimplification (and to be simple is no problem for me), let me suggest that there are at least two basic factors involved in the beginning of drug abuse. One is the influence of the peer group (for both teenagers and adults) and the other is the availability of drugs.

Incidentally, what's the best way to become an addict?

To know one.

Here's something else that usually knocks people down like a row of dominoes: The age of first drug abuse is usually between eleven and thirteen. (At that age I was still looking for the prize in the Cracker Jacks box!) The age of first heroin use is between fourteen and sixteen. (By that age, I had found the prize. I just didn't know what it was.)

And so you're thinking, Oh, but that's got nothing to do with me. If you're thinking about the Cracker Jacks, you're right, but if you're thinking about drugs, you're wrong. Dr. Walter Leman, director of a teenage rehabilitation program in Norfolk, Connecticut, has stated that every young person is a potential drug abuser, and he doesn't have to have emotional problems to push him on the bandwagon. He had some words of advice for uptight parents, those who are worried about what young people are exposed to these days. (And that includes most of us.)

Dr. Leman's advice bears consideration. Here it is:

First of all, let your young people dress as they please the majority of the time. Of course, you don't want them running around in dirty clothes, all beat up, (the clothes, hopefully), and looking like refugees from your friendly neighborhood dogfight. But most of the time, try to play it cool and let them dress their way.

Next, he suggests that teenagers be allowed to wear their hair any way they want to. This might be a tough pill for some parents to swallow, but it's better than other pills some of the young people are swallowing, if a choice is involved.

You know what really breaks my heart? The hurt of a young person who doesn't know that his parents care. Often it's not the down-and-outs who find themselves in this sinking boat, it's the up-and-outs. They may come from families with all kinds of money.

I remember a young man, sitting there in his sleek Grand Prix and fighting to keep back the tears. "Don't tell me to go home and talk with my folks about it . . . they won't even know I'm there. I've been home a lot since my buddy got picked up and my girl left town, but they haven't even noticed. They don't even see me as a person—don't tell me to talk to them!"

And I didn't.

That teenager—the child that's yours or the one you influence—he needs to know you love him. And how can he, if you never touch him?

Dr. Leman's next point was just this. He decried the practice of many fathers who never touch their sons. An arm around the shoulder or an affectionate pat on the back speaks volumes. Touching someone has a personal something to it that is so much sweeter than just sitting across the room and mouthing words.

I've always been the kind of person who had to reach out and touch someone. It may be just a pat on the shoulder or perhaps just putting my arm around someone's shoulders, but it gives such a warm, wonderful feeling.

Another point is respect. We expect this from our young people; should we not give it as well? They are crying inside to be recognized as persons, as individuals, rather than simply as projections of ourselves. A whole volume could be written on this.

In a certain sense, a whole volume has. It's called the Bible. It's a love story. And love is the basis for this whole business. "Love one another."

Dr. Leman indicated that the drug abuse problem deals with the whole person, and hence, the treatment does also. That is, the approach found to be most effective is an overall one. The program tries to meet the total needs of the individual. A three-pronged approach is utilized: To help the individual face reality, to help him with his moral standards (teaching right from wrong), and to nurture him in his spiritual development.

Such an approach is a "far piece" from where we have been in the 60's and 70's: "Let everyone do his own thing in his own way, however he wants to. Who is my neighbor anyway?"

In the last few years we have lived with ideas like this permeating much of the fiber that structures our existence. And the result? More people are broken down mentally and/or emotionally than ever before in the history of our country, of our world.

What does this say to us?

Dr. Leman's approach is a clarion call to the setting of standards, to the re-affirming of certain ideals that give a young person something to hold to. Or, to put it another way, it is a twentieth-century approach using New Testament thinking. The Scriptures tell us that standards do exist, that there is right and wrong, and that each individual must come into the right relationship with the God who loves him.

Let's look at some of the drug facts as set forth by Dr. Leman. Marijuana may not be physically addictive, but it is psychologically addictive and that's far worse. New users today include not only our high school and college youth but also those in junior high and even in the elementary grades. For the drug pusher, younger children are all too often pushovers, unless we as parents and interested adults warn them of the dangers.

The situation is sad beyond words, because some of these lovely young people will blow their minds and their bodies and there will be no one around to wave a magic wand and say: "Have you blown your mind? Here—have another one!" Fairy godmothers pretty much went out with Cinderella, but some of the rest of us are still in danger of turning into pumpkins if we don't watch out.

If the marijuana user smokes pot several times a week—say perhaps three times—and keeps this up for a period of three months, he enters what doctors call the "no care syndrome." Changes in the personality occur, but they are seemingly so subtle that the user himself may not be aware of it nor is his family.

One of the bad aspects is that the user feels he is accomplishing great things, although his performance may be well below potential. Marijuana, in the beginning, may make the user talk with less inhibitions, but then he also cares less. Additionally, it lowers inhibition.

Incidentally, speaking of performance reminds me of an interesting test series that was run along these lines. Six rock music groups were tested. Each group cut a tape when they were high on marijuana and then a second tape when they were straight. They gave these two tapes to qualified music critics who judged them on their performance. The critics agreed that the tapes made when they were high were technically incorrect and inferior to the one made when they were straight.

A further interesting commentary is that the members of this group were asked to judge their own tapes. They were given the tapes when they were high and picked out their "high tape" as being best. Then they were given the tapes when they were straight and they picked out their "straight" tapes as best. We hence conclude that drugs do not help a person function better; the problem is he *thinks* he is functioning better. Unfortunately, this is not all in the mind—it seems to be all out of the mind.

I was also interested in learning about a test or a series of studies done in London regarding brain damage and brain atrophy as a result of using marijuana. Such tests indicate that the drug does indeed alter the chemical balance of the brain.

People who use marijuana (sometimes called "Mary Jane"—and isn't that a horrible thing to do to a nice name) almost all start because they want to relieve tension, to "expand the mind," or perhaps just to see what it's like. After using it for a while, they are bored with it and find that it requires more and more to reach the same kind of high that was first experienced. At this point, rather than continuing, some people say, "Forget it." These are the ones who do not go into hard drugs. But the others who have entered the "no care syndrome" have a tendency to go on. Of course marijuana doesn't force you to become a part of the drug scene, but you are less strong in your decision-making and there is a tendency to go ahead and take some new drugs. Thus, the involvement with drugs such as LSD begins.

One of the true nightmares associated with drug use is the flashback. I don't know if you've ever seen one or been around anyone who has had a flashback, but I have. Never in my life have I seen anything so horrible.

I was visiting with a lovely young friend of mine, sitting in her room talking one night. Some two months before our visit, she had accepted Christ as her Savior and had asked him to come in and make her life over. At that moment she had stopped taking drugs. I recall that as we sat there she said, "I have not touched anything, marijuana or anything else, since I became a Christian." She paused a moment and then she added, "I feel so good and clean and wonderful."

And in just a few moments she had a flashback. It was one of the worst things I have ever experienced, beyond my powers of description. I had thought up to this point in working with young people that nothing could surprise me nor shock me. I was wrong.

When this precious girl came out of the flashback, she looked up at me with tears streaming down her face and said: "But, Marge, what's going to happen? I haven't had drugs for two months. How long will this go on?"

I was sick on the inside because I did not know the answer. I could not tell her. No one could. With some people, flashbacks occur rather often; with others they're farther apart; with some they stop; with others they don't.

Statistics show that when a drug abuser gets to LSD and similar drugs there seems to be no turning back. Six months later, the user will be on heroin. Without it, the individual feels he can't sleep, he can't eat, he can't function. He feels like his body has stopped, but the motor (which is his mind), is running full speed. That feeling

is one of the symptoms. The user is on the scene but just can't get
with it. He knows he has to have heroin. When he has a shot, he
seems to get better. He sleeps, he eats, he's in high spirits, in every
sense of the word, until that shot wears off. Then he's back in the
same boat, and it's leaking.

Heroin is sold by the bag, approximately 1/64 of 400ths of a grain
of the white powder wrapped in tiny little cellophane bags. Beginner
users will start with the dose of a single bag of heroin, already di-
luted or cut with something like talcum powder or milk sugar. He
will pay from five to ten dollars for each bag, and it may be as little
as 5 percent pure heroin. Hard-core addicts require up to thirty
bags for a single dose and need several doses a day. Can you imagine
how much money that takes?

LSD, the common name for Lysergic Acid Diethylamine, was
first synthesized in 1938 by Dr. Albert Hofmann, a Swiss chemist
who was looking for a drug with which to treat migrane headaches.
It is a colorless, tasteless, odorless liquid that is usually taken by
mouth after being poured over a sugar cube or in a cookie. (I believe
I'd prefer some other type of icing if you don't mind.) It belongs
to a group of drugs called hallucinogens. All of these have one thing
in common—they cause hallucinations—seeing something that isn't
there. (Here I'm on home ground. For years I have imagined that
I am a gorgeous and fascinating creature, but neither my mirror nor
my friends seem to verify this.)

There are other hallucinogenic drugs such as peyote, obtained
from a cactus plant. (I thought I had some of this for sure the first
time I tried making cactus candy. Later, someone told me I was
supposed to take the thorns out.)

Marijuana, although classified with the narcotics for many years,
is really a hallucinogenic drug also. It is smoked as a cigarette,
called a "joint" (and has no reference to the place where the
cigarette is smoked.)

Since the promoters of drugs claim that the use of them is
"mind expanding," they appeal to some young people of college
age and younger, trying to free themselves from a generation which

seemingly does not understand them and apparently lives in the past. It seems to me that the claims that drug pushers make bear strong resemblance to the honey-voiced medicine man of other days: "This will cure stomach trouble, lung trouble, heart trouble, arthritis, acne, dandruff, and the seven year itch."

It sounded great; it just wasn't true.

Claims made today that a drug is "mind expanding," that it gives new insights and capabilities—these are simply not true either. On the contrary, the ultimate results according to all tests include panic, sustained shock, disorientation, unresolved psychoses, and thoughts of suicide.

As parents and workers with young people, we must be on our guard, never assuming, "This can't happen to us."

Heroin, or "H" as it is sometimes called (along with other names like smack, horse, or junk) is an opiate, along with morphine, codeine, opium, etc. These are the most widely used hard narcotics.

Heroin is a major problem in ghetto sections of metropolitan areas. The number of juvenile heroin arrests and overdose deaths is moving sharply upward, according to TANE (Texas Alcohol Narcotics Education). Heroin is a semi-synthetic derivative of morphine, and comes from the unripe seed pod of a certain species of poppy.

The usual method of taking heroin is by "mainlining," shooting a liquid made from the powder directly into the blood stream using a hypodermic needle.

In addition to the drugs mentioned, there are also depressants such as barbituates and amphetamines—"pep pills." The latter have been on the market since the early 1930's and were used to treat colds and hay fever. Then there is methedrine, also called speed, dexidrine, and similar things.

From time to time we hear discussion about the possibility of legalizing marijuana. Dr. Leman made a specific statement along these lines: "If marijuana is legalized there will be a tendency to legalize everything else." And then he asked this pertinent question, "Why should we take the kid away from reality?"

His feeling is that legalization would decidedly be a step in the wrong direction and would result in a tremendous increase in the use of marijuana. This thought seems to sum up the situation: There are many minuses regarding the use of marijuana, and I don't know of one real plus.

There is one more drug that is rarely mentioned, but is just as deadly and "sneaky" as any that has been discussed. This is the liquor problem. The young people speak of it as "booze." I suppose the reason it is so frightening to me, is because as a young girl, I was exposed to it and its deadly results and miseries! My brother and I grew to hate it because we could see what it was doing to our father and how much unhappiness it could make in a home. So I grew up with a terrible hatred of liquor, beer, or any facsimile of it. As Chuck, my husband, and I worked in the area of business, we saw a nonchalant attitude toward it develop in the minds of most everyone we knew. We became so "used to it" (although I never could even taste the stuff) that it too joined the other items in the "gray area"—neither black or white, just gray!

It is frightening today, however, to realize that this is not just a minor problem now; it is of major proportions among our young people, and they are not the only ones. The social drink today is as acceptable in modern society as a glass of milk or a Coke! And much more sophisticated! And cool! We are so brainwashed by advertisements showing neat young people draped over a sparkling glass of beer or a drink, and captions stating: "Only for the coolest people!"

I keep remembering the young people I am called to help or talk to; they're draped over something, too. But it's a rest room commode, or a chair, or on the floor, or in a bed in the hospital! To see some of these kids—and they're just kids—so sick and so pitiful, and to know that many of them will end up alcoholics or near-ones makes my heart break. They're not all older teenagers, some of them are not even out of junior high school!

One day I was talking to a high school student and he said: "Mrs. Caldwell, last night my dad came home late from a party with Mom, and he was staggering drunk. You know what he said to me? 'Son, don't ever let me catch you smoking that pot. You leave that stuff alone.' "

This young man looked at me and asked: "Mrs. Caldwell, what's the difference?"

I replied, "None at all, Son," and thought of the father who was talking out of both sides of his mouth! What kind of influence would he have on his son, saying one thing and living another.

The reason the liquor problem is so deadly, as I mentioned before, is because it is so acceptable in our society. Hardly a function can be held today outside the church, without a "happy time" before. And we'd be foolish to say that there are not those who can "take it or leave it alone." But which of us knows who will be the lucky ones? I guess it is on my mind so much because I deal with it so much in the lives of the young people in my work. I ask the young people on every campus, both high school and college level, what they think the number one problem is today among their peers. Without any hesitation they all tell me it's the booze. In the last few years since drugs have been so rampant, many young people are beginning to see the horrible results and are leaving it alone. But in its place comes another drug that is causing misery and illness, even much addiction, among our young!

Those who have studied the complete drug picture have some excellent suggestions for fighting the problem, which can be considered along with Dr. Leman's ideas. They suggest that a good place to begin your responsibility to your children is to closely examine the atmosphere of your home, to be sure that there is a feeling of belonging, a feeling of acceptance and time for each other. Families seem to have fewer problems who spend enough time together to know each other, to understand each other, and to have a high level of agreement.

It's also good to "accentuate the positive" as we used to say. We can talk in terms of individual growth (hopefully upward) and all the avenues open to us here. Let's not emphasize the negative, simply telling young people they must not do this or that.

As adults, we are all too often much better at speaking than at listening. I remember the experiences of a friend of mine with her teenage son. In his elementary and junior high days, the family was so busy with so many activities (and all of them good) that there wasn't much time left for family life. (Certainly it is true that these are busy days, but the time which we do have as a family unit needs to be spent in sharing with one another. Sometimes the quality of our time together can make up for its lack of quantity). The mother looked back and remembered that she had not kept pace with the boy in allowing him to be an individual. In his teenage years, she was still in the process of imposing her ideas upon him during the little time they had together. The result was that he shut her out completely. When she had something important to say, he simply didn't hear her.

"I have been so painfully aware," she said, "that during those days I did an awful lot of speaking and very little listening. The result was that communication broke down and later when he really needed me, there was just no way that he could hear me."

There is also much merit in the idea of discussing the drug problem openly, of getting accurate information from reliable sources, and talking over the situation as a family.

Christianity, of course, plays a major role here, both in preventing the problem and in curing it when seemingly the case is hopeless. Many, many instances are on record like that of my young friend whom I mentioned earlier—drug abusers or perhaps just drug users— who found the Lord as personal Savior and let him take care of the problem.

Some other interesting information is reported which indicates that students with religious affiliations consistently report less drug experience than those who have no religious affiliation. Additionally, it has been found that students who describe their parents' religious experience as deep were less likely to report drug experience.

"What's wrong with smoking a little pot?"

Everything! Run away as if your life depended on it. It may.

13
"Marge, I Have a Problem..."

Because of the nature of my program, I receive a great many letters each week. These letters reflect the loneliness, sickness, rejection, depression, and general unhappiness of so many people in this world. Each letter could represent thousands of people who are suffering in the same area. Sometimes my heart just breaks for people: the utter loneliness of so many located in the big city and not knowing anyone to turn to; the young women moving into the city from smaller towns and fearing to walk outside their apartments because of the dangers they have heard about and the depression that comes to many of them as they try to fit into a life-style that is so alien to their lives; the frustration of the homosexual who so desperately wants to be accepted into straight society; the teenager who is experimenting with drugs, and finds too late that to blow your mind and body is the most desperate of them all; and those who are terminally ill and blame God in one way or another for their plight.

Where is the answer? Why, oh why? Who can help me? Where do I turn? Who *really* cares whether I live or die? These are the cries I hear endlessly from these letters and phone calls! And in my heart I know with certainty that I *do* have an answer! My answer is not some little cliche that has been used over the years, not to "grit your teeth and try to hang in there." My answer is not to find an avenue of escape so that you can pretend that the problem isn't there (some think that by pretending long and hard enough, it will go away), nor is it a type of religious "high" and "low" that makes you feel that you are on a psychological see-saw. My answer can be found in a Person—a "born-again" relationship with a living Person. This Person is Jesus Christ!

Jesus Christ never said that he would keep us from problems. If we accept his loving salvation, which, incidentally, is free, he comes to reside in our hearts. We use the term *hearts* because in the New Testament they spoke of the heart in this way. However, Jesus works in every area of our lives that we will allow him the freedom to operate in. It is with our *will* that we decide whether or not we will ask him in. It is an exciting thing to me that the great God of the universe who made you and me and gave us the privilege of thinking for ourselves and a will to do what we choose to do—that wonderful God does not treat us like robots and force us to do what he wants us to do!

Because he loves us so much, he wants the very best for all of us. He has a plan for each one of us! He is the master architect, the creator of all the universes, yet he made you and me in his image (with a will and spirit). How can you fathom that? It's too magnificent to grasp! Since he made us, who would know better what it took to make us happy?

The truly exciting thing to me is that God gave us some guidelines in order to help us live this life he has for us! Now, think back! In your family when you were growing up, did your parents make some rules that you liked and some that made you boiling mad? Did you think to yourself that they (rules *and* parents) seemed illogical and stupid? Did you rebel at some of them and then at a later date you saw how glad you were that your family "stuck to their guns?" Did you think at some time in your young life that your parents just made those rules to keep you from having a good time? That's the way we feel about God's guidelines, isn't it?

I've thought sometimes that God *must* be sitting up there on that little white cloud looking down at me saying something like this: "Ah! Ah! Don't do that! That's fun!" or "Ah, *ha!* Now I've got you!" or "You missed my will again! Keep trying!"

How wrong we are! Jesus said he wanted us to have an abundant life, to be happy and full of joy, no matter what happens to us in this life! He tells us some ways that he can help us do just that. And you know what we do? We yawn spiritually and say that we don't really believe the Bible or we don't have time to read his love letter to us or we're too busy to think about it. Or we just shrug our shoulders and look sad and resort to a life of confusion and frustration, and, as a result, many of us fall into the trap of self-pity! "Why is all of this happening to me?"

Most of these problems can be identified in the category of "culture shock." When we become teenagers, we enter a world that is completely different from the one we've been living in. We leave the sheltering arms of the family, so to speak, and become neither a child or an adult. That is beginning to happen at an earlier age in our modern society, however. Then we have new and exciting, yet frightening feelings and impressions enter our minds and hearts! How can we cope with them? What can we depend on as a "leveller"? Who can help us? Well, if we have nothing to go back to in our subconscious mind as a gauge of morality, we find ourselves struggling and slipping into the "slime of the new immorality." We feel very ignorant 'way down deep, so we look up one of our peers who feels the same way and exchange our ignorances!

There is the "culture shock" of our living conditions. We've lived one way at home or on the college campus, and now we're thrown into a huge apartment complex. My soul! You could die and be dead for a week, and no one would know or care! Everyone comes and goes, no one speaks, and you see things happening that you feel repulsed over! Your mind begins to wonder if you'll *ever* begin to understand this new way of life. And if you ever understand it, do you want it for your own?

Where are the ideals and the goals you have set for yourself? They are beginning to fade a little, and you feel like a naive, little child in this new "culture." You don't want *anyone*, but *anyone*, to know what's going on in your mind, so you try to act real cool and sophisticated. Down deep in your heart, you're full of confusion and frustration, and sometimes a terrible sense of guilt sets in. That's the worst of all! Then following the guilt comes the depression and the inability to cope with your emotions! Then the desperate search for someone or something to assuage your mind and body!

Another "culture shock" moves in on some of you. This is the world of drugs and booze! I think this area causes more suffering than all of the others put together! Then there are some who turn to the area of sex. There are those who think: I must prove something to myself, I don't really know what, but something! You go from one sex partner to another, always looking for that something or someone who will satisfy you. There are those who argue against marriage—that it takes the zip out of your experience with one another—and then you find yourself sick and crying with disillusionment over the situation you're left in! "Try it, and see if you're suited! If not, then just get out and try somebody else!"

Oh, the list could just go on and on. And I so desperately want to help you find your way back! So with no apology I recommend Someone to you who knows where you hurt and loves you no matter who you've become or where you've been! He never shakes a finger at you; he waits patiently for you to come to him or to come back to him. He wants to forgive you, cleanse you, and give you a new life. His name is Jesus, and I have found by personal experience that I can depend on his consistency, his love, his concern, and his forgiveness. But I have learned another way, too. As I counsel with numbers of young people and adults alike, I thrill as I see them turn to a Person. I have seen this Person free them from drugs, teach them a new life-style, mend their broken hearts, give them new interests, and give them hope when they didn't want to live any longer. How could I have seen this happen over and over and not truly believe that Jesus can do just what he said he would do? It's thrilling and exciting to watch him in others' lives. I *know* he is the answer to your problem no matter what it is!

For this reason I want to share parts of some letters that I have received. I have selected these because they best represent the many others that I have. The first one is from a college senior.

"Marge, I want to write and let you know what's happened to me! Last week I made a new commitment with God. I really can't tell you whether it is the initial one of asking him to come into my life, or whether it is a reevaluation of what I had done at an earlier age. Many of my friends think that it was a deeper commitment on my part. It's very hard to explain, but I do know one thing that is for sure! Something did and has happened inside. The important thing is that my name is written in the Book of Eternal Life.

"My mom and I sat down today and tried to talk. You remember I told you that we never got along and couldn't communicate at all. She thinks that these four years of college I've completed have been a waste and have left me worse off as a person than when I started. I tried to explain to her today some of the things I've come through—the guilt, the punishment I've inflicted on myself, and the hangup I have about showing affection. I don't think I could make her understand completely! She may *never* understand, but I know now that she does love me, and I've tried the best I could to make her know "me." It's thrilling to me to know that she loves me anyway, and I was afraid she wouldn't. I'm beginning to see a different lady now that I call Mama. Now that I'm beginning, with God's help, to lose the bitterness and hatred that I've lived with so many years, I'm finding in her qualities that I didn't know existed. And I have a desire to know her better. It's that great! It's one of those miracles of love to me, and probably the very best thing that could have possibly happened!

"My roommate at college is in a terrible state of mind. Because of her basic insecurity, she has run from one sex experience to another. It leaves her exhausted emotionally and psychologically. She is living with a terrible guilt, because she knows that down deep she is doing something awful to herself. I've never seen anyone so desperate, and she needs help. I talk to her whenever she wants to talk, but since I am not experienced as to how to advise her, I'm not much help. I did share with her, however, my experience of last week, and she just cried and cried. She said it seemed to her that God would never forgive her, and that she felt like a hypocrite, running to him when she was down. I told her that that was certainly the time to run to him. But she does need help! Will you help her to find her way?"

Another letter comes from a young adult who lives just outside the city. She had tried everything and faced only an emptiness and void whereever she turned. She heard my program one evening, and several weeks later wrote me this note:

"Mrs. Caldwell, I've wanted to write so many times and tell you what has happend to me! So tonight I decided I would not let one more day pass without doing it! Several weeks ago I heard your radio program (quite by accident) and you were talking about what Christ can do in a life given to him. I began to think about my life, and how I'd wasted so many years. You told how to ask Christ into your life, and what he would do if you'd give him freedom to do it! All of a sudden I saw myself like he must see me, and I was almost physically sick! I did ask him to enter my heart—it wasn't any great prayer because I just don't know how to pray. I just asked him to forgive me and help me, and I cannot tell you how all the guilt and ugliness lifted! Each day seemed better than the last. He doesn't waste any time showing you his glory either! I've had so many miracles happen to me already, and it's just been a few weeks! Your talk that evening really penetrated my wall of resistance, and I'll be forever grateful! It's so hard to put down in a letter all that I feel because I've surely felt an overflow of love that I never thought possible for me. The Lord knew what time I'd be ready for him, and with the help of others I was led directly to him! I'm going to close now, Marge, but I just wanted you to be a witness to my salvation!

This letter came as a result of a program on homosexuality. I received many letters and calls as a result of that particular program, and this one represents them all. I had read the first chapter of Romans in the New Testament, giving God's opinion of sexual perversion. I had also read from a documented article as to the frustrations in the gay world, which was written by a homosexual himself. Out of twelve years of counseling I have found that there are few, if any, homosexuals who are completely satisfied with their lives and would choose that way of life over again. But the most important thing is what God has to say to the homosexual, and no amount of rationalizing can change that!

"Dear Mrs. Caldwell: It puzzles me that I feel I should write in response to your program on homosexuality. What about those who accepted Christ before they fully realized their true homosexual nature? Such is my case, and I'm not ready to accept the fact that God doesn't understand my dilemma. Is the only Christian option remaining for those like me an obligatory celibacy and chastity? Inasmuch as the sex drive is God-given and my sexual orientation is certainly not of my own making or choosing, I think not. In contrast to the author of the article that you read on your program, I have been much more relaxed among my gay friends than I ever was when I was awkwardly trying to make my way in a straight world. You would be surprised if you knew how many outstanding young men in the business world are homosexuals. I count many of them as my dear friends: physicians, dentists, and other professional men, persons with intelligence, education, dignity, and self-respect whom you would no doubt be delighted to know. And it is from this vantage point that I stand and refuse to say that God doesn't understand."

A high school senior writes:

"Dear Mrs. Caldwell: I work part-time in a hospital, and it is really terrific. But I do have a problem, and it worries me. These people need so much love and kindness, and especially spiritual help. And I feel so bad because I can't give it to them. When you've been away from God for so long, you can't just jump up and supply that help. It seems especially hard when you go to a school and kids cuss so much, don't talk about anything very long except dope, alcohol, sex, etc. Then you come home to a father who could care less about you or what you do. You get to a place where religion won't help, and you don't have any friends you can talk to. And then, well, it's just hopeless at times! I know that I need to get back to church and that I should change, but I don't know if I can do it! I've changed so much in the past few months that sometimes I hardly know me anymore! And I'm miserable. Please help me! I want to have that feeling of love that I used to have. Marge, when I lie down at night, I cry so much and those tears are of loneliness. I didn't used to cry like this, but there's a great big empty space in my heart now, and I want Jesus to fill it again. Please write and tell me how I can find my way back to God."

This letter comes from a wonderful young man in the university, a sophomore student. He was an agnostic and very much steeped in what he was supposed to believe. He is very intelligent, a super student, and to top it all, very handsome physically. Soon after he accepted Christ (after weeks of searching honestly, and coming to the conclusion that Jesus was real and the Bible was true in a glorious way), the Christian girl who had been so concerned with him and was responsible for his finding help, was taken away.

"Dear Marge: A few weeks ago, as you know, the whole world had seemed to collapse on me. I had more on my heart than I could hope to cope with. The question for me was where to turn. I had accepted Christ as my Savior and sincerely too, but did I now have the faith to trust my life to him? I never could grasp what Susan had always tried to help me understand, that I must submit my life to his will. Now I do. "It's like a treaty. A treaty is only a piece of paper until it

too is tested. Likewise, was my faith only words until it too
was tested. Let's face it. It is easy to believe when everything
is going just fine and admittedly not so hard to praise the Lord
in times of minor hardships, but when someone or something
that means the world to you is taken away it is hard to reach
out to the Lord. Especially so when you feel it is he who has
taken your "life" away. On the contrary, if you reach out to
him you find he can give you the "life" bought by the death
of his Son, but only if you have faith—faith that what has
happened is in his will for you, and that all this has strengthened
you as a new Christian. I finally realized this. Marge, until two
weeks ago I only witnessed to one person and I failed because
I was talking. In the last two weeks I've witnessed to three
people about what has happened to me, and I felt a new life
in me everytime (I used to think talk like this was nonsense).
That's when I noticed the sculpture. I fashioned it the day
after my spiritual birth, July 26. Why? I don't know, but it
has existed since then. I looked at it just yesterday and realized how much of a carnal Christian I really was. I had accepted Jesus, I saw the Way, but I never took the next step.
Now I have, Marge. Above all, I realize now that what happened to me has strengthened my faith. The new life it has
created in me is beyond words. Please pray that I can rely
on Christ to pull me out completely, and that I can be a tes-
timony to others. Now, more than ever, I realize it's one
thing to *say* what one believes; it's another to *live* what one
believes!"

One day I received a letter from a lady in her fifties who had been
listening to the program, and she wanted to share how a new hori-
zon had opened to her since her acceptance of Christ, and her growth
in a prescribed Bible-reading program that I had shared with her.

"Honestly, as God is my judge, I am not imagining this! I
really don't 'feel' like I used to before, or let's say, when I first
learned about Christ! In looking back, I had *such* ugly

thoughts. I drew my skirts, so to speak, if people didn't think the way I did. I was so very uptight about too many things and people. I can't put it *all* in words. Last week I realized what an impact love could make on my relationships with others, and as God filled my heart with love, I honestly couldn't believe it! Now when I meet a friend that doesn't seem too friendly or seems preoccupied, I quickly pray that God will help her with her problem. There was a time when I was so full of *myself* that I would have reacted much differently! Through the study and application of biblical teachings I have outgrown ever so many childish ways, and praise the Lord, I am learning the true joy of adulthood."

Another letter comes from a young adult who listened to my program on premarital sex and what God has to say about it.

"First, in regard to premarital sex, what do you propose for the thousands of single men and women in this country, cold showers? Do you really believe that a so-called blessing from a preacher or the state makes the human sexual need legal and moral? Sex is for sharing between two people regardless of church or civil blessing. A great many single people achieve a great deal of physical and emotional satisfaction from sex, and that is more than some married couples can say, based on the increasing rates of extra-marital relationships and divorces in this country. Who set you up as the authority to judge anyone's morality, or lack of it, regarding anything? Please don't quote the Bible because although to your way of thinking, it is the ultimate authority, everyone does not accept it as such. The right to decide one's own sexual commitment to another human being, and one's own ethical conduct in everything else for that matter, is a very personal one, and is hardly subject to anyone's judgement except that of the two people involved. I am sure that God does not wish to deny single men and women life's most beautiful and personally rewarding experience merely because they have not signed some papers and submitted themselves to the prescribed religious or civil rituals.

"You mentioned that Christianity has the only living Savior. Why don't you concentrate your obviously fantastic energies on the hypocritical Christians running loose, clean your own house, and leave the Moslems, Hindus, Shintoists, and the rest of us heathens, as you would no doubt call us, to our own beliefs? You certainly have the right to believe what you want. More power to you. But don't impose your beliefs and so-called morals on the rest of us; give us dissenters the same right we extend you. Your statement that Jesus is the only one Savior that is alive—did it ever occur to you that Allah, for instance, is just as alive and well to Moslems as Jesus is to you? Otherwise the entire world would have been Christianized long ago, with no Crusades, no Inquisitions, no mass slaughter of the "infidel" in the name of Jesus. Your exclusion from salvation, whatever that nebulous term means, of the disciples of the other great religions of the world, some much older than Christianity and born from much greater civilizations than that of the first century holy land, is hardly a charitable or Christ-like attitude.

"I would sincerely hope that you will find better things to do with your life than prattling on about the immorality of pre-marital sex and the conversion of nonbelievers in an half hour, or an hour, or whatever. Sincere religious conviction does not come that easily, Billy Graham's crusades and you notwithstanding."

There were more letters, and phone calls, as I've told you. Some of them were very bitter as the one above. Some were very sweet—some in agreement, and some in vehement disagreement. In one letter I was called the "Anti-Christ," and in another one I was called "the sensuous woman." Chuck said he didn't want to live with the anti-Christ, but he didn't mind the "sensuous woman!" And we both fell out laughing! I have laughed and cried, but mostly I have prayed that God would use this radio program as a vehicle through which he may reach as many people as possible! When I read or hear the words, "Marge, help me!" my heart goes out to that person. And my prayer is that God will fill that heart with himself, and heal that body, mind, and soul! Our problems can be the steppingstones to a victorious life!

14
"The Fool Hath Said in His Heart"

I want to sit down and talk eye-ball to eye-ball with you. We're in my den, and there's a great, roaring fire going in the fireplace. The room is dimly lit, warm, snug, and it's snowing outside! We're comfortably dressed, and so glowy inside and out! We've just had a dinner of steak, potatoes, salad, and strawberry shortcake and . . . you ought to be ashamed! Look how stuffed you are! And I'll *never* eat again! I *always* say that just after a large and delicious meal!

We've been discussing the problems of our day: the Watergate crisis, the trouble in the Holy Land, Vietnam, drugs, booze, the whole bit. With a great sigh of discouragement, you have just asked me what can possibly be done, and what's the use anyway? What's it all about, and why does it have to be this way? You have just said that you didn't believe there was a God, but if there was, why didn't he do something? And when I mentioned the Bible, you just pooh-poohed it. You said it probably was written by a bunch of "psyched-out" promoters who got together and said, "Let's get this together; we could have a good thing going!" You really had to admit, you said, that they were some kind of promoters, they had caused quite a stir! The last thing you said was that you really didn't think God was alive, anyway!

I tried to talk to you from my heart, but you wouldn't listen! I prayed so fervently in my heart while I was talking, that the Holy Spirit would help me reach you; it was important to me to help you to see! But I had to keep remembering that the Bible told me to be patient with someone who did not understand spiritual things! And I was so frightened! I wanted to just tell you to open your mouth (spiritual, that is) and let me force-feed you until you understood! But, of course, that's impossible, and we wouldn't want it that way anyway!

I'm so excited that the wonderful God who made me and made you, gave us a will—the ability to make up our own minds. That's how we're made in his image. He doesn't do that, and then deseciate that privilege by forcing us to do something against our will.

Well, you're gone home now, and I'm sitting here about to cry and thinking about how I blew this opportunity for the Lord, and with you, my dear friend!

How I wish I'd said this, and how I wish I'd thought of that, and why didn't I reply so-and-so? So, do you know what I'm doing? I'm sitting here in that same room, the same fire, the very same full "tummy," the whole bit, and I'm pretending that I'm still with you! The only difference is that I'm writing you some things that I think you will appreciate. I just couldn't get them out in the right way. I'm pouring my love and heart into this letter, hoping that you'll receive it like I mean it—with love and concern. It's because you don't have to go through life wondering if there's a real God, you can know assuredly! You don't have to doubt the validity of the Bible. God said: "Heaven and earth shall pass away, but my words shall never pass away" (Matt. 24:35). (I can just hear you saying, "But I don't believe the Bible, so what he says doesn't help much.") I'm going to give you some facts out of the secular world that will make you stop and think!

The Bible is so exciting! It's a combination of books with a central doctrine, plan of salvation, and one rule of faith. Just think! It was written by about forty different men over a period of as much as sixteen hundred years. Now that's something! And listen to this! It was written in three different languages, Greek, Hebrew, and Aramaic. It was also written by men who lived in three different continents: Europe, Africa, and Asia! These men were so different! They were princes, poets, philosophers, fishermen, statesmen, prophets, priests, publicans, physicians, educators and shepherds—their style of writing and thinking had to be different! The writings of some of the Scriptures occurred almost fifteen hundred years prior to the birth of some of the other writers! And when you think where some of the writings came from! In cities, in the country, on deserts, on islands, in jails, and in some cases, in the palace! Some of it is poetry, and some prose, some are letters to the churches, and some of the most beautiful parts are written as parables! There is preaching and allegory. Now, isn't it almost an impossibility that a book written like this in these different places, under such different circumstances, languages, and cultures could become one complete volume? But, you know, that's exactly what happened!

Let me tell you something else interesting! The Old Testament was written in Hebrew, with a small portion written in Aramaic, because this was what the people spoke at that time. The New Testament was written in Greek, the language used in letters and writings of that time. Greek was understood and spoken in the world of that day, just as English is spoken all over the world today, although it may not be the first language! Many people didn't really understand the ancient languages of the Scriptures, and you know what happened! Different versions and translations began to appear, and still do, in languages spoken all over the world. I know what you're thinking! Since there is a gap between the time that they wrote it back there and we got it, how reliable is it? Or you may be thinking, Is it more reliable than the other writings of ancient times—or is it *really* the truth from God? If the fellows who wrote these books were inspired of God, were they intellectual giants who were able to write in such a way that we got it from them *correct* after eons of time had passed? Heavens, no! When we look at them, they were just folks like we are! But they *all* said they were told by God to write these things down, even though they didn't understand what they were writing! This is what's so important about their writings in comparison to other ancient manuscripts!

I have heard people criticize the Scriptures by saying that the gap between the time of the writing and possession of a complete manuscript was too many years. But let me tell you something! We accept the manuscripts of the philosophers of ancient times without question, and hundreds of years, even thousands, have passed since they were written. Only 100 to 150 years passed between the time of writing and the possession of the writings of the New Testament!

Do you remember the findings of the Dead Sea Scrolls in 1947? We had a lot of excitement about this because it erased about a thousand years gap between transcriptions of the Old Testament Scriptures! In 1947, a young shepherd boy had lost one of his sheep in the area around the Dead Sea among the caves. He threw a rock into one of the caves and heard some pottery break. To his amazement, as he looked in, he found pottery jars containing ancient scrolls! The accuracy of these scrolls when they were compared to the Bible were absolutely hair-triggering! One scroll contained a complete text of Isaiah in Hebrew among them. *Exactly* as we have it today, with some very minor language differences? The scholars who investigated it all came to the conclusion that the text from Isaiah found in the cave at Qumran had actually been copied about 100 B.C.

The Bible has never said it was a book of science, yet it never contradicts science. In fact, science is now proving what the Bible has said all along. The Bible just claims to be a lovely love letter from God to man, reaching out to him and desiring his love in return! But the science of archaeology has daily begun to prove what the Bible has been saying for ages! Let me give you an example! In Genesis 11:31, we read: "Then Terah took his son Abram, his grandson Lot (his son Haran's child), and his daughter-in-law Sarai, and left Ur of the Chaldeans to go to the land of Canaan; but they stopped instead at the city of Haran and settled there" (TLB).

Critics of the Bible have been in doubt as to the accuracy of the biblical account. They claimed that Abraham was probably an ignorant nomad and very primitive with no knowledge of commerce, business, transactions, and so forth. No one knew anything of Ur of the Chaldees; so we said it was probably a myth! In 1923 in Mesopotamia, near the Persian Gulf, archeologists uncovered a whole city—and wonders of all wonders—it was the Ur of Chaldees! Just like the Bible said! Isn't that something? And the funniest thing! They found receipts for business transactions, formulas for math problems, clay objects that were books. And can you imagine, payrolls for female employees! I wonder if we'll find that they had their version of Women's Lib in that day? So you see, Abraham was proven to be just what the Bible said he was! They concluded that he was the product of a brilliant culture, and indeed, it did take a lot of faith for him to pull up stakes and go to an unknown land!

Up until this century, people laughed at the biblical fact of a people called the Hittites. They are mentioned forty-six times in the Bible. Critics said that no such people existed because there were no secular proofs of their having lived on earth. Yet the Bible said many times and under many circumstances that there were such people. In 1905, the critics stopped laughing! In the hills of Ankara, Turkey, some writings were found! When they were translated, the unbelieving world had to admit that the hitherto unknown Indo-Germanic Hittites and their vanished empire had indeed existed!

I guess I get most excited when I think about prophecy of the Bible and how it is being fulfilled right before our eyes in our day! I used to say that if I could choose a time when I would rather have lived, I would have loved having been here on earth at the time Jesus lived and walked on earth. But I've changed my mind! I would probably have been like Thomas. Remember him? He reminds me so much of myself! He was the disciple who doubted! But I have too, and I think I would have been capable of saying just exactly what he said! Remember when Jesus had appeared after his resurrection to the disciples? They were so excited about it, and Thomas hadn't been there. When they told him, he said: "Man, I wouldn't believe that unless I could see it with my own eyes, and touch those

places in his hands and side!" This is the version according to
Marge!)

I'm so glad Jesus gave Thomas a chance to see for himself, aren't
you? That makes me take heart! I'll always remember what Jesus
did! He came one day when Thomas was there, and appeared before
him. When he asked Thomas to feel the scars, Thomas didn't have
to touch him! He just fell down on his knees, and cried: "My Lord,
and my God" (John 20:28). I get excited when I think what Jesus
said next. "Thomas, because thou hast seen me, thou hast believed:
blessed are they that have not seen, and yet have believed" (John
20:29).

That's you and me! We haven't seen and touched him, yet in faith
we can believe that he is! And how God does honor faith! Yet, in
our day, the prophecy told of in the books of Daniel and Ezekiel
in the Old Testament are coming alive if we'll just recognize them!
The land of Israel, the upheaval in the Holy Land with wars and
rumors of wars, the direction that the Common Market in Europe
is taking, the world system of churches, the world system of mon-
etary values that we are adopting, the common language, English,
that is being spoken, the whole moral decay of not only our own
beloved America, but the world, the confusion in the minds of all
people, the violence and crime, earthquakes, and floods—*all* of these
things are spoken of in the Bible and are prophesied by God through
the prophets! Billy Graham has said that if leaders of the world
would only read the last book of the Bible, Revelation, they would
almost *know* what is going to happen next!

Remember when the apostle John wrote the book of Revelation?
He had been exiled to the Isle of Patmos for proclaiming Christ.
So out there in the loneliness of that island, God told him to write
down some things that were going to happen in the future! Now,
John wasn't superhuman! He was inspired, sure, but he had a lot of
curiosity too! He kept telling the angel who was speaking to him
that he didn't really understand what he was to write down! The
angel just told him to write, that he didn't need to understand!
Don't you know John felt foolish when he wrote down that during

the time of tribulation that 250 million soldiers would descend on Israel? There weren't that many people on the face of the earth at that time, much less in one nation. But isn't it interesting that in a national magazine a couple of years back that China boasted that she could put an army of 250 million on the field at that time? Not 150 million, but the same amount that the Bible mentioned? The Bible says that in the latter days the land of Israel will bloom like a rose! Well, we wouldn't have to see many pictures to know that this has happened with the cultivation of those arid lands!

In the tiny little book of Micah in the Old Testament, we read that the Messiah will be born in Bethlehem, Euphratah! Now, what a coincidence that Jesus was born there, when logically he should have been born in Nazareth where Mary and Joseph were living. Mary was hardly able to travel by donkey at nine months, don't you think? But she did, because the Bible said she had to be in Bethlehem!

They always thought that the earth was flat and talked about the "four corners of the earth." Then in 1492, along came Columbus and confused us all by telling us that you wouldn't fall off the earth if you got too near the edge because the earth was round after all! Now, if we had seriously read the Bible a long time before Columbus, we would have known that the prophet Isaiah told us that the earth was round in his book, chapter 40, verse 22. He told us that God "sitteth upon the circle of the earth."

I will never forget a friend of ours named Allen. When we lived in West Texas, Chuck and I worked with young people on Sunday evenings. We had a fantastic group of them and had some great discussions during that day on God, man, relationships, dating, and everything in the world that was troubling them. We shared some evenings, and all in all, I think we touched a nerve in our spiritual lives quite often. One evening Chuck and I were in our department all alone because it was quite early. A young man walked in, introduced himself, and asked if this was where the young people met. We assured him that it was, and we began to talk. He was from Pittsburgh, new in Texas, working for an oil company, and had his PhD in geology. Besides all that good stuff, he was driving a beautiful convertible, which didn't hurt a thing with the girls! All the young people took him in and made him feel very welcome. Sunday night after Sunday night he came, and then one Sunday evening it happened! Chuck and I came to the church quite early, not realizing that it was so early. When we discovered what time it was, we almost left the department, but bless Chuck! He just sat on the side of the table, and we had one of those great times of sharing! Lo and behold, here came Allen!

"I don't know why I'm so early," he said, "but I just didn't have anything to do so I came on."

Down deep in our hearts we felt maybe we knew why he was so early! We had been discussing Allen and wondering about his spiritual status. So he began talking, and it all came out! He had made great grades, was really very intellectual . . . and logical . . . and had found no time for God in his schedule. Besides it seemed to him that if you got involved with God that you had to leave your intellect and will outside of your life. He really felt no need for God, and classed himself as an agnostic. He just "let it all hang out" and shared all his feelings in an honest way! But we did notice that he was very honest with himself and us. We began to see that if he were truly a skeptic, at least he was an honest one, and we could go from there! He asked if he could talk to us privately, and we made a date for the next week. He came, and we talked into the wee hours of the morning, and then many times after that. We asked if we could pray for him, that God would touch his heart, and he told us that he needed all the help he could get!

One night he called and came by. He sat down, and after a little while, he said: "Folks, I just wanted you to know that earlier tonight I asked Christ to forgive me and come live inside me, and be my Savior."

We cried, hugged each other, and cried again (at least *I* cried, Chuck just sat there and gulped and choked like men do because they're not "supposed to cry"). I asked what *really* made Allen think seriously about the claims of the Bible and Christ on his life!

I think what he said might help you, because it has made so much sense to so many since then. He thought a minute, and then replied:

"Well, many things made me think! You see, I never believed the Bible was true because I'd never given it much serious thought really. I just chalked it up with what I'd heard other people say about it, and I'd never checked it out. Nor had I checked out the people whose word I took without question. I didn't even know what they really knew about it. In other words, it was like one ignorant person (biblically speaking) asking questions of another ignorant person, and they just exchanged their ignorances. Then another thing! Those prophecies that have been proven by history and are *facts* written hundreds of years before, well, how do you look facts in the face and refuse to believe them? I couldn't get around that! My mind is trained to think logically and when you proved to me that I could have a logical mind and accept so much of *fact,* that Christ didn't expect me to ditch my mind when I accepted him or my intellect, that made me stop and think, too! But I guess the most powerful thing that I just couldn't get around was the love and concern in the hearts and minds of all these young people up in that department! And you folks! Why did it make so much difference to you that I believe? I couldn't get around that either! And your prayers! How I thank you for praying for me!"

So another young man, an intellectual young man with his PhD, another Nicodemus (you'll find him written up in the third chapter of the book of John) found that faith and fact can live in the same heart of an individual. He found that Christ gave us these minds, and he wants us to use them for his glory! And you know what's so interesting to me? And exciting? God works in our intellect and is active in our will because that's where our *real* decisions are made! I'm so glad I'm not saved by the way I *feel!* Some days I feel close to God, and other days I don't *feel* so close! Some days I *feel* spiritual, and others I don't *feel* anything! My emotions and feelings don't determine my state of salvation, and I thank God for that!

It's so late, and I'm so sleepy! My eyes are getting heavy, and I think I'll call it a day! But just know that this was written to you with love! My earnest prayer is that God will use it in your heart as he did in Allen's—that you will find the peace and joy through Jesus Christ that can be yours for the asking. Jesus is real—he's not willing that any man should perish, but that all should come into a saving knowledge of God through himself. He said that he is "the way, the truth, and the life" (John 14:6). Ye shall know the truth, and the truth shall make you free" (John 8:32). So I wish all of this for you, my dear friend!